MW00532296

BARE

BARE

wounds, wisdom,
& worthiness

Niccole Nelson

Bare by Niccole Nelson

Published by Inspired Girl Books
Asbury Park, NJ
www.inspiredgirlbooks.com

Inspired Girl Books is honored to bring forth books with heart and stories that matter. We are proud to offer this book to our readers; the story, the experiences, and the words are the author's alone.

The events are portrayed to the best of the author's memory. While all the stories in this book are true, some names and identifying details have been changed to protect the privacy of the people involved.

The author has tried to recreate events, locales, and conversations from her memories of them. In order to maintain their anonymity in some instances she has changed the names of individuals and places, she may have changed some identifying characteristics and details such as physical properties, occupations, and places of residence.

The conversations in the book all come from the author's recollections, though they are not written to represent word-for-word transcripts. Rather, the author has retold them in a way that evokes the feeling and meaning of what was said. In all instances, the essence of the dialogue is accurate.

The author and publisher do not assume and hereby disclaim any liability in connection with the use of the information contained in this book.

© 2022 Niccole Nelson

All rights reserved. No portion of this book may be reproduced in any form without permission from the publisher, except as permitted by U.S. copyright law. For permissions contact: help@inspiredgirlbooks.com

ISBN: 978-1-7373163-8-1

Editorial and Creative Direction by Jennifer Tuma-Young

Cover Photo by Allure & Soul Photography
Cover Design by Vanessa Mendozzi
Typesetting by Roseanna White

Editing by Laura B. Ginsberg

Library of Congress Control Number:
2022943715

⚠ WARNING:
TRAUMA TRIGGER WARNING

To remain integral and authentic I wanted to give a disclaimer to the branding that is me. My story is my brand, and that may come with some triggers. I know some of you have heard some portion of my story while others have not. There is as much, if not more, trauma as there is triumph in my story, so by all means if reading any portion of my book brings things up for you that you are still on the journey to healing flip past those pages or close the book altogether. I appreciate your purchase, however the most important thing to me is that you are safe, seen, heard, and true to yourself first. Please take what you need and leave the rest for what you need on your journey to wholeness. I completely understand. I pray that you find your way back when that tender spot no longer triggers you.

GRAMMAR DISCLAIMER

I write like I talk. My artistic expression may not always be grammatically correct. However, my intent is that it is thought provoking, honest and at times entertaining. My hope is that you see beyond what some may deem incorrect and find the value in what's being shared.

DEDICATION

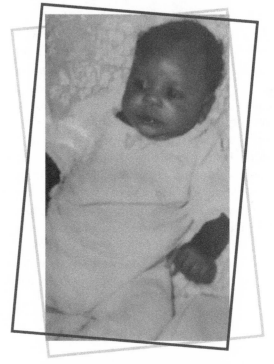

This book is dedicated to CoCo (my younger self).
She is the reason I pray the way I do.

NOTE FROM THE AUTHOR

"The wound is the place where the Light enters you"
— Rumi

Now I'm using that Light to show others the way through their tunnels.

When you're in the pain and discomfort it's difficult to see, hear, or feel anything close to a way out.

I believe you've come across my book as your guidepost to healing and to overcoming the things that have (or had) you hiding in the darkness of your pain.

Our darkness can be a mere shadow, some small residue left by heartbreak, betrayal, or a poor decision we made. In other cases, that darkness can be an attic, a place where we've tucked all our darkest secrets and hidden hurts that shame wants us to keep. This only keeps us from showing up fully in the world as God intended. We may have a beautiful life, successful career or some small variation of what we believe a wonderful life is, but God wants us to have a life of abundance.

Now, when I say abundance, I'm not just talking about material things, titles, or a big bank account. I'm talking about a fulfilling life.

No more striving for anything: recognition, validation, or wanting to be liked. This life is prepared with greatness and strength. You're now thriving, as well as confident, aligned, and intentional about how you show up in the world. This is a life of purpose. Living on purpose, with purpose.

What's purpose? Well, God described it to me this way.

Purpose: when you and God have a secret and the only way you can tell it is by living it out.

I know, right!

I cried the first time I wrote this on a page.

No one else has your purpose.

People believe purpose is only what you do, when, in fact, it's who you are more than anything.

It's your je ne sais quoi: a quality that cannot be described or named easily.

It's the, *how you do it*, that no one else can do quite like you.

What does this have to do with your wounds and the Light?

In order to live out your purpose, share your truth, and be authentic, your wounds have to be cleaned, and that stings, most times. Healing can be exhausting and often more painful than the hurt itself. However, there is no recovery without bringing your truth to the Light. I'm baring mine in hopes it will encourage you to do the same.

FOREWARD

KENYETTA M. CAMPBELL

Hebrews 4:13

Nothing in all creation is hidden
from God's sight. Everything is uncovered
and laid BARE before the eyes of him
to whom we must give account.

B.A.R.E.

Being Able to Reveal Everything!

Telling the NAKED truth about a woman, who bares her soul to the world and proves that you can bet on yourself and beat all odds.

"This book is about to change lives, while breaking inter-generational curses. Niccole's bravery in navigating the cards that she was dealt is shocking, intense, and transparent."

-Kenyetta M Campbell

Niccole Nelson, "The Girl Next Door," is a dynamic, fierce, & detail-oriented community leader, writer, and survivor that has been instrumental in transforming Detroit!

Our friendship sparked nearly 40 years ago, living two different life experiences, with just a driveway separating the both of us.

I've had the pleasure of watching Niccole conquer her goals by not allowing her circumstances to interfere with her growth. When I reflect upon our friendship, I'm reminded of our similarities and differences. I was blessed to be raised in a two-parent household, whereas Niccole was adopted. At the young age of 12, I didn't realize how much she had gone through until our paths crossed years later. At that time, I realized that she is by far one of the strongest women that I know.

While playing with Barbies, baseball in the street, and jumping fences to have a little summer fun, I was clueless of what Niccole was struggling with. As we approached high school, there was an obvious change in her behavior. She appeared to be promiscuous, but excelling academically and in sports. We lost contact after graduation. I went off to college, and Niccole began working at the post office. She still managed to become financially stable in her early 30s and successfully raised her children as a single mother.

Buckle your seat belts because her story is about to heal women all over the globe. Sexual abuse, mental abuse, physical abuse, abandonment, unhealthy relationship, single parent, reunited with her birth mother, then losing her in a tragic accident. Niccole now stands to show the world that if God has a calling on your life you shall survive.

I was blessed to connect back up with Niccole after introducing her to the community work in the neighborhood we grew up in. This was by far such a blessing in so many ways. The Girl Next Door became my boss, and together we have successfully raised over $20 million in our old neighborhood. My fondest memory of Niccole's involvement in community work was watching her advocate for foster care children in Cody Rouge. It was during these meetings when I would hear her repeatedly share her story. Each time I would learn something new that brought tears to my eyes. I was clueless to the depth of what was going on in her life growing up right next door.

Watching her conquer the burdens of life made me realize that if you are determined to succeed and have a strong connection with GOD you will be able to stand the test of time.

Reading this book will encourage every woman that has ever felt burdened by unworthiness to be unapologetic in laying BARE her truth and letting go of shame and use her voice, while helping others heal. Niccole shares her trauma and rebirth in a way that made me realize, others need to hear this story. We all can benefit from witnessing her growth, resilience, and transformation. This book will touch the lives of so many people who will be able to relate to her journey.

Signed,

Kenyetta M Campbell,
The Girl Next Door

CONTENTS

XVI | PRELUDE:
Past, Present, and Purpose

3 | LETTING MY HAIR DOWN
*The pinned up mental blocks from abuse
and the stamina it took to push through.*

31 | UNBUTTONING MY BLOUSE
Revealing my heart, how I overcame
self-inflicted betrayal being in and giving love.

105 | REMOVING MY BRA
The significance of deep wounds and the scars.

119 | SLIDING OFF MY PANTIES
Who got in them and how, the emotional and (mental) effects of each experience.

141 | TAKING SHOES AND SOCKS OFF!

Ordered steps are not always pretty just like feet.
Doesn't mean they weren't made by God, your destiny awaits,
first step is to heal, next is to help.

163 | DROPPING ACCESSORIES

There will be titles, toys and traditions that may look nice and
at times make you feel the same way, but they are not the core
of who you are or what you were put here to share (show off)
so be sure not to get thrown by the glitter and glam, but
instead be sure God is getting the glory.

173 | RINSE AND REFLECT

*Showering you with love as you clear your heart and mind
of who you thought you were so you can step into
who God called you to be.*

Prelude:

PAST, PRESENT, AND PURPOSE

It was subtle, almost like a whisper
He came in with a gentle caress to
    rescue me
His love was a bridge over my tears of
    pain
Fashioned by the dysfunction,
    deception, and turmoil of my
    childhood
As I looked down at the water shed
    from my pain
I knew the one who would never let
    me thirst again had kept me
The weapons chosen to destroy me
Molestation, rape, verbal, mental, and
    physical abuse
Were no matches for:
Daily word, faith, prayer, praise, and
    worship
The more of me He revealed
At His feet I sit in tutelage

With the water of His wisdom pouring
    over me
I am shown my likeness to Him
The unwanted, discarded girl
Had now found her beauty courage
    confidence and strength embodied
    in His love
My fight was no longer my own
But for those coming behind me who
    would long for the same love
To educate and edify were now my
    orders
To march in His army
Not as a cookie-cutter soldier
But as the outside-the-box
    communicator of the message
    instilled in me by my creator
My forgiveness has given me freedom
Which I use to put my life on paper
To show how He took my pain and
    turned it into greatness

Letting My Hair Down

THE PINNED UP
MENTAL BLOCKS FROM ABUSE
AND THE STAMINA IT TOOK
TO PUSH THROUGH.

METHODS

All healing (mine) and breaking (with God) will not be done in the church (house) or by traditional methods. Don't let others, or your own perception, hinder the process by boxing God into whatever and however you think or have been told the change has to or will happen.

I was three months out of homelessness living in the exact house I prayed to God for. All the details I put in my prayer/vision book for the home I wanted, while living in one room, in a hotel with my teenagers. Except it was in the city. Yes, where I vowed I wasn't moving back to. I was in love with the suburbs and never wanted to move back to the city. What I didn't know was the work God had planned for me to do in the neighborhood where He had my house. Yes, the very neighborhood I grew up in, I would come to run as Board President and change for the better. Sometimes you just don't know what parts of your life are the most significant to His plan and your story.

My landlord is a retired employee of ours that has a few homes he rents, and one had been broken into some months prior. I was asking him about that house and if he'd gotten it secured and any of the items they stole replaced. He politely said that he would rather not discuss it because it was too painful. Then he started to tell me about another house he owned. Not once had I said I was looking or that I was homeless. In my head I'm saying, *I'm not moving back to the city. Why am I wasting his breath and time?* He went on though. Then he said, you should come by tomorrow before work. Without hesitation, I agreed. When he left my office, I shook my head and thought, *Girl you know you ain't moving to the city. Especially over there.*

Needless to say, I saw the house. He lived across the street, so we went back there to discuss things because his grandson was napping there. He asked if I liked the house. I did. You want it, he asked. I began to tell him how I didn't have money saved, not sure how long it would be before I'd have move-in cost. Blah blah blah. All the things we start to share to disqualify ourselves when no one asked.

He said, I didn't ask you that. Do you like the house? I said yes. He said go tell your kids y'all moving today and handed me the keys.

Of course, I cried. Four carloads, between me and one of my girlfriends, me and my kids had a new address we still call home six years and counting.

God doesn't need your help or input on how to meet your needs nor does He keep from you what's necessary to change your circumstances even when you don't realize it's what's best for you. The change He made in my life, May 2014, allowed me to impact thousands of lives for the past six years as Board President for the top CDC in my city.

It's incredible how pivotal surrender is to our success in living out our healing while in His will.

ONE JOB

You have a responsibility to you
to be whole.
— God

SURVIVAL SHIFT

Today I realize that survival mode is us trying to help God out, when He is taking care of our needs, but we think we need to be doing more.

He's trying to get us to thriving, but we, most of us, have been conditioned to survive. We just doing what "we" believe is necessary to gain ground in whatever we are trying to accomplish. If we would stop doing long enough, we would see and hear who He needs and wants us to just be. In that being is the doing. The doing is alignment. Aligning His will with our work in purpose. In the thing He's called us to.

We're no longer striving, which by definition is strenuous. The Word says, "The blessing of the LORD, it maketh rich, and He addeth no sorrow with it." (Proverbs 10:22) Rich to me doesn't only mean financially. Rich in life, in family, in experiences, and in all things.

Sustainable holistic wealth. Wealth that can only be measured by the person living in it. Your bank account isn't the only marker. Nor is it any status symbol you've purchased. This is the thriving era. The moments, the impact you're making in the world and the relationships you've nurtured over time. Those are the markers you leave on your path that both you and God will look back on as the most memorable as well as ones to be most proud of.

Thriving in and of itself is to be fortunate, successful, and flourishing. This is the abundant life God promises, and I'm gonna enjoy it just like He intended. Now I know faith without works is a very true statement, but when you align your practices and daily effort toward the intended result with God's will, that is your faith in action, that is the works.

FAITH WITHOUT WORKS IS DEAD

We think the "works" are the things we must do to prove our faith, but today God says, the work is changing your mind around what He desires of you. The work is becoming new. The unlearning of old mindsets and habits. Not your plans of what you think the road is to where you want to be, but to shift perspectives of how He is going to do what you have asked of Him.

Faith by definition (biblical) is the substance of things hoped for, the evidence of things not seen. (Hebrews 11:1) Now when we really look at this scripture, how can something not yet seen be evidence at the same time? The work you're doing, renewing your mind, cleansing your heart to see His perfect plan for your life versus you striving for something He may not even want you to have. Or worse, that would bring you destruction.

It's not only how we see a thing; it's also how we see ourselves that becomes most important. The faith, the evidence, is in the trust in yourself to become who God can use in the position He's called you to. Who do you have to become to walk out this assignment in this season?

Over thinking limits our faith. I have been asking the question, is over thinking unbelief? If you're making things up before they happen, if at all, are you even consulting God, let alone trusting Him. Is your faith in

His ability or your own? In these cases, the work is being worked up, not productive or purposeful. Your mind is so clouded with your fake scenarios, you'd never have clarity around what your next move (works) is anyway.

Drowning yourself in preparing so you never really actually have to move is not faith. That's called shrinking or hiding behind planning. Ask me how I know. You can't be waiting on God and walking by faith at the same time. The work is within most often. We can't control outer elements. People, outcomes, all the things that have outside variables is up to God and His timing. You are the only one who can control you.

Get in the mirror and do that work. Your faith in Him will increase and shift the odds in more of your favor. You will begin to see you and your life in the way God sees them both. Don't let shame, unhealed trauma, self-doubt, or fear keep you from the abundance that God has for you by working the wrong muscle as it pertains to faith.

WHITE NOISE

What does quiet look like to you?
When you slow down
When you ground yourself and quiet the noise of life
Where do you find yourself?
Are you sitting on a beach in the distance
In a park near a trail
In your favorite comfy chair sipping tea
Currently I am in the parking lot of a beauty supply
I've been sitting here for about ten minutes since I
    made my purchase, feeling the amazing breeze on
    this spring day

I read a quote on Marshawn Evans Daniels' Instagram
    just now
"A shift requires aligning with the unforced rhythms of
    grace" (Matthew 11:28–30)
It resonated with me on a cellular level
I stopped to take it in, and this was the question that
    came to mind

What does quiet look like to you?

How do you feel when you sit with it?
I've been practicing driving in silence
Yes, no music, podcast, or phone conversations

Just me and God on the road. Except I'm not praying. I
 just wait to hear Him speak
I don't have any expectations, just wanting to be present
 and available for His prompting
This is me working through and out the conditioning of
 using distractions as a coping mechanism
I used to wear my headphones, one because I love
 music, but more so to drown out and hide from my
 stepmother.
Pain was made bearable by each beat
Every lyric was a lift up out of what I was living in
What was once a safe haven, is now a habit of avoidance
 and distraction
I only discovered this when I noticed myself always
 saying, "I need the noise." The white noise. I don't
 need it. I just enjoy it. That's only because it was a
 comforter.
So as I journey through the silence, I am finding my
 way to a stronger more intentional me
In the quiet I am finding the best version of me

KNOWING

Knowing the lesson is one thing.
Getting it is another.

OLD NEWS

You're so busy replaying the tape of old issues and past hurts you can't hear God calling you into your healing.

Instead of seeing what is true for you now, you're living the nightmare of yesterday. What you're missing is keeping you there.

A **rerun** or **repeat** is a rebroadcast of an episode of a radio or television program. There are two types of reruns – those that occur during a hiatus, and those that occur when a program is syndicated.

A "repeat" is a single episode of a series that is broadcast outside its original time slot on the same channel/network.

Your life is a series of events. Yes, it may even be a movie. However, you are not on hiatus, nor are you syndicated. So playing back the reruns of times past for more than a reference of how far you've come is pointless. All it's doing is keeping you stuck in a season of your life that God is no longer in, and who wants to be where God was? Nobody, that's who.

Getting about the business of living in the moment. Being in the now breeds innovation and creativity. Taking God out the box and allow the full expansion of your dreams to be revealed one incredible season at a time is the only way to produce more of the same.

The repeats are nice for a time. A time to reflect. To

see how the technology of you has evolved. Your mind doesn't thrive off those things anymore. Your habits have changed. For the better, we hope. Your friends, and the places you frequent, have all taken on a resolution that has brought about a mature clarity. You are no longer on the same wavelength that you once vibrated on.

There is a progression that you should be working toward. Instead, you're stagnant. God is streaming live new data, and you want to remain on VHS or Blu-ray. I know it hurt. I know you'll never forget how they (or it) made you feel. No one is asking you to. I'm asking you to use it to write a new script. To seek out a new cast in the story that is your life. Come back to the future and write it in your favor. See and share the value in the purpose the pain possessed. Don't let it paralyze you. Don't let a moment or moments become a life sentence. It is a part of the story that makes you who you are, it's not what you are.

You've been given a mantle to share firsthand accounts of things some don't live through. Help someone else survive their trauma by shedding light on how you healed yours.

FAKING IT

*You pretended to be ok for so long
you started to believe it.*

MOUNTAIN MOVER

God's power within is the power I am connecting to, that is propelling me into my purpose

Just wrote the above statements as I'm watching Mel Robbins' talk about how she believes in signs and is asking the audience what's their next chapter.

I immediately thought about the mountain I'm facing, being something I'm back at and she puts on the screen:

"Your doubts create mountains. Your actions move them."

CRAZY!

There are situations and circumstances that are out of our control. Others we build, one small scoop of conditioning or bad habits at a time. There are moments in our lives where these meet, and that mountain we may go around, like the children of Israel, for years.

My self-made mountain garnered the title "Homelessness."

We make decisions that put us in jams, and then God uses those decisions to teach us valuable lessons. Lessons He believes will keep us from repeating the habits and decisions that got us there in the first place. Other times we experience things as a visual example for those watching God move in real time. We usually find that out after the circumstance or situation has been resolved. Most often it's after a friend or family member tells you if they hadn't seen you go through what you just went through, they wouldn't be able to make it through a similar situation.

What happened you ask? Well, let's say this mountain is made of snow, because like building a good snowman, the more I rolled with it, the bigger the problem got. You know when you roll the snowball until it's a bigger snowball? Yea, like that.

We were moving from the city to the suburbs. My son picked up the apartment book and said, "Mommy we should move here." It was a beautiful apartment. We called the town Stars Hollow, from *Gilmore Girls*. Fast forward several years and memories later, life, illness, and not using a budget took me down roads I never want to experience again.

My oldest daughter, who has Sickle Cell Anemia, had been hospitalized for some time. I had to miss work with no leave for a few weeks. Among other bills, I fell behind on my car payments. In my not-so-infinite wisdom I thought, well I have to pay for the car to get to work, to pay for the rent that's behind. Have you ever been there? Robbing Peter to pay Paul? To not paying anybody at all? Oh, just me? Ok.

Unfortunately, my robbing Peter to pay Paul method didn't work, and I lost my truck to repossession. So what do you do? You take the next paycheck and get a new car. Well, at least that's what I did. In this moment, let me tell you. Do as I say, not as I did. Because all that did was push me even further behind with my rent. I would get a burst when I paid some of what I owed, but I was still behind.

Now, I am working on my terrible habit of not asking for help. In this mountain-making moment, I did just that. I swallowed my pride and went to the one place I knew would either help me or direct me to someone who could. I went to MDHHS and applied. It wasn't that I thought I was above the support from what some unaffectionately call welfare. It was my internal self-talk that I should've been able to manage my money and life better, so I didn't need the help in the first place. I was ashamed of my choices, not of having to go to the welfare office.

Any who, back to what is turning into a too long story. LOL. DHHS decided they would help me. To my surprise they even called me on a Saturday to confirm all the details. If you know anything about them, you know they ain't open for clients on Saturday. So, I knew God had smiled on me that day. Fast forward to the day my payment was to be wired to my leasing office. I had paid my portion of what I owed and once the DHHS office wired the remaining balance I would be all caught up.

Well, here is where things went completely left. I had told my kids we were good. All the information was in, and I would see them after work. So imagine my surprise when my son called me to tell me the sheriffs were putting our things on the curb due to nonpayment.

Yep, we were literally on the street.

In a panic I had to tell my boss I needed to leave work early and why. As I rushed to what used to be my home, I called my case worker to tell her the disturbing news and find out what happened on their end. When I finally got a hold of her, she screamed, "They can't do that."

I said, "Oh yes they can, because they are." I am outside watching my kids grab clothes from the lawn and put them in our car. We were officially homeless.

Of all the offices in Michigan, my social worker said they had a transformer blow up and the building caught fire before my payment, or anyone's payment, could go through.

Just like that, thinking I had done all I could to prevent this moment, God himself said I have other plans. Usually, we want and think His plans are going to be glorious, fun, and beautiful with a favorable outcome. Well, at least what we envisioned when we prayed for the answer. In God's eyes this is the blessing. Learning.

I know God has put everything I need to move my mountains inside me. Like every other human being in the world. I also know that when you are staring the mountain down it makes all that power seem like it has shrunk.

If you can relate, I'm glad you feel seen. Keeping our focus on Jesus. This is the only way we can move any mountain.

MENTAL STIMULATION

The sight of him was yummy
Some may even say delectable
But when he spoke
I found his words...to be
Hors d' oeuvres from the platter called intellectual
I thought it would be the same lines
Fed to me by guy after guy
Time after time
But he was unique in his approach
See...he was coming for my mind
Through my ears
He entered my cerebrum
Like a ballerina
The words
Danced from my ear drum
His dialect
Penetrated the center of my nervous system
Causing me
To be suspended in his wisdom
His thought process
Ingenious
Damn!
He even has goals and aspirations
His conversation
Gave a girl hope

And inspiration
To hold my attention
Rather than the organ between his thighs
To my surprise
His verbiage stimulated arousal
In the one behind my eyes
The diction was a massage to my cerebellum
That infused every muscle in — my — body
We agreed, disagreed, grew, and laughed
Never a dull moment
Nope...no gray matter here
This dialog had painted a picture
Of literary elegance
For my cerebral cortex
It did things for me
Beyond physical sex
As his words hit my medulla oblongata
Down to my toes
Ran a tingling sensation
Our conversation
Was good
I thought of it as...mental masturbation
This man's intellect
Had taken my brain cells on a fantasy frenzy
And
By the time it was over
My brain wasn't the only thing that needed to be
    washed!

MEDICINAL

Meticulously cleansing the wounds of your past with
    my heart
I wrap them in sincerity and honor
As the scab of trust forms never to be picked at in the
    healing process
The scar of hope left to remind us to continue to love in
    spite of pain
The gashes of the past oozing the blood of torment
Infected by those who tried to hinder your future
Sterilized with the betadine of prayers
And stitched up with forgiveness
To free you of the infection of their lies
The blow dealt to your mental state
Was devised to take you out the game
To render you unconscious and leave you comatose
Instead you flipped it
And created an escape of verbal exit wounds
You allowed your pen to cut away the cancerous liaisons
Trying to form growths on your intelligence
The present cuts burning from alcohol
Of truth pouring over you to create courage and
    strength
The self-hatred from mistakes and mishaps cleansed by

the peroxide of purpose
Foaming to show direction on the road of scraps and
    bumps
On your way to destiny
As life evolves and develops
There will always be bumps and bruises to be tended to
There is nothing to gain from licking your wounds
And dwelling on them
But growing from them as the bandages unravel
To reveal the greatest part of the healing and a stronger
    restored you

REALITY CHECK

I've fantasized my entire life. I believe it was to escape my poor reality. That realization is only fully forming now as an adult, though; I'm not sure if I knew that as a kid.

I've carried this with me into adulthood. Maybe it distorted my reality to shield dealing with my trauma.

Maybe it wasn't romanticizing but fantasizing that kept me from the reality I've desired.

It's weird though because I always face and overcome my harsh reality.

It's all ironic.

Reality can be too painful.

Sometimes you miss the beauty in the world by being literal.

It's funny how writing about myself is helping me see new parts of me as well as old parts differently.

Maybe all my fantasies were just dreams that couldn't wait until I was asleep.

Writing this book is the therapy I never had.

POWER DRIVER

Why am I afraid of my own power?

I sat with this question — I mean literally sat and meditated on it, using it as a mantra.

What came to me is, I am afraid of the new me, or should I say the real me, that has to show up. And the not knowing, the uncertainty, the loss of — or what I believe is the loss of — control.

I've been so conditioned to shrink that showing up fully is unfamiliar to a point where it feels wrong. What I want is so emotional to even write down. I'm in tears just writing that I need to write down my desires.

It's more than the not knowing. For years, and even today, I never believed I deserved what I desired. So I stopped dreaming.

It's like the work I will have to do to go back and get that girl will be so emotional that I shy away or build a wall so I don't have to roll the stone away and see the residue of my past.

When in reality it would be just that, residue. Dust I can blow away and discover or rediscover the joy and the uncensored me. The girl who fully, blindly trusted God even before I knew Him. The girl who believed her current pain was no match for Him.

The molested little girl who didn't understand why it was, but knew it was, wrong. Who carried burdens bigger than the smile she hid them behind. The smile was her shield held up by shame. The shame would lean on pride and judgment to rest. Or what appeared to be rest. These bedfellows were not for the outside world; they were all my own.

Pride — not asking for help when it's clear I needed it. Then judging myself for even getting in the situation in the first place. Then Shame comes, picks up the shield and says smile, it will all be ok. We'll deal with it when we get home. All the while you're (me) sitting next to the very person who could've helped at the first sign of trouble.

See, Power doesn't always just mean strength as in strong. It also means courageous and wise. Using your wisdom — knowing you need help. Courageous — using courage and asking for the help when you know it's beyond your ability.

Now this power also embodies the ability to see beyond circumstances and tap into the God living on the inside of you.

This power, when sought after and tapped into daily, will help you avoid situations before help is needed. Some circumstances are growth spurts and lessons, but other times you have all you need to move the mountain, change the trajectory, and shift the atmosphere all on your own.

Purpose will push you, and, if you haven't found yours, this power will guide you to it.

THE LIGHT

People say, don't let anyone tell you...

What someone tells you is not the issue. The problem is if you believe it!

What you believe, you become.

I was told on a regular basis that I wasn't gonna be nothing.

Or I'd be a dope fiend like my mother.

Even though now, I know my stepmother was projecting and in pain herself, I still wonder why she looked at me and I triggered her hurt. I mean, she took me in. I didn't ask to move in her house. I know on the surface it was greed that drove her desire to foster, but just looking at me at times would make something click, and I became a target. It could've been what I was wearing, my decent grades, me smiling just for the sake of joy, and she would fire off some type of insult.

I felt so many emotions growing up in her house. Now, for her I feel sad. Birthed or borrowed, either child, she had enough turmoil to dish out to us all.

I often wonder if it was the sheer fact that no matter how hard she tried she could never destroy my light. It may have flickered a few times, but never went out. This reminds me of a time she took me to her church. She had begged and begged, "Don't you wanna go to church with me? Why don't you wanna go?"

Based on who she was and the "spiritual" practices she had, I didn't know Jesus at the time, but I knew what she did, and whoever she worshipped, I didn't want no parts of (it). In true Ms. Nelson fashion, eventually I was told, I'm going to church.

So, the next time she went, me and my baby girl were in tow.

The church was very dark. A sign already that this ain't where I wanna be. The pastor or leader, I'm not sure what he was called, came out once we were seated. My stepmother was on the end of the pew. I sat next to her, and my baby was in her car seat next to me. Now most people when they see a baby, they want to get a closer look, ask you how old they are, is it a boy or a girl, etc... He walked the main aisle and looked at my stepmom, and I then looked away immediately. Not even a hello visitor or cute baby. I was told later that he told her to get and keep me out of his church and never bring me back there.

I'm not sure if it was my light and or power he saw. I just know he knew both our "spirits" couldn't be in the same place at the same time. Needless to say, I was never asked about church again.

Maybe my stepmom hated my light too. Based on the things she said to me and how she treated me...maybe she knew she needed that light but didn't know how to ask for it.

Writing this now I wonder what my life might have been like if I had the knowledge of God, courage, and compassion to offer the light. To ask about her life. Who was she before the hurt took over?

Unbuttoning

My Blouse

REVEALING MY HEART,
HOW I OVERCAME
SELF-INFLICTED BETRAYAL
BEING IN AND GIVING LOVE.

SILENT KILLER

Today in prayer I asked to be the version of me God
    sees
I went into the spiel mentally, physically, and spiritually
Better body, mind, and heart
It led me to thinking the number one killer among
    women is heart disease
How we sacrifice our hearts for others
Does this increase our risk?

PROM NIGHT

When my prom date gave me this picture, I teared up. Looking at it always brings up so many things. Then God goes and asks me, "What does she deserve?"

She wasn't only frail, she was fragile. She didn't know it then because she was tough on the outside. She was a survivor fighting her way through the pain. She was already someone's mom at 17, praying to get back to her own.

I want to hug her. She deserved to be loved. Cared for in a way that would feed her talents, nurture her confidence, and give her the courage to keep dreaming. Instead, she became a chameleon fading into the background of her circumstances.

It's the breeding place of my shrinking for others. Looking back, I wonder if I picked this red dress as a distraction from pain subconsciously.

Even back then she had the ability to capture her audience. Whether at professionally talking with secretaries at school or performing one of her musical talents. Most of all she loved to dance. So to be able to go to prom after being pregnant for 9 months was an amazing moment.

She deserves love
She deserves to be whole
She deserves peace
She deserves love
She deserves joy
She deserves to be seen
She deserves to be heard
She deserves to be valued
She deserves love
She deserves abundance
She deserves beauty
She deserves fun
She deserves celebrations
She deserves friendships
She deserves love
She deserves freedom
She deserves grace
She deserves respect
She deserves laughter
She deserves to be vulnerable
She deserves honesty
She deserves trust
She deserves love...

SHIPS PASSING

Timing in a relationship

You two may be meant to be, but not now. You know, like when lovers meet but get back together years later?

It's like a boat restoration. No matter what condition the boat is in, it's still a boat. However, if it's in need of repair, it won't float, so you can't be in it. The only way to repair it is to get out of the boat, fix what needs to be fixed, then you can float on.

Is it the person or love that eludes you? Well, me. I can't say I've ever had the experience of the one who got away. Some memorable one-night stands, yes. Anyone I am pining over to return, not so much.

I am, however, a hopeful romantic. I love love. It is the affection, attention, and intimacy that drives my desire for companionship. Communication, honest communication is a must.

The boat for me is love. Not an individual. My boat unfortunately has holes, torn sails, and a tattered rope on my anchor. Holes in my theory about what men really want from me based on the stories I tell myself about my past. Those old tapes on repeat that my self-talk keeps on shuffle in my mind. Torn sails that I need God to stitch up, so I have some direction on which to float until my mister arrives. I had let my broken heart deflate the wind I needed for it to be opened. Never being able to anchor myself to anyone from choosing the wrong men to dock at my port.

The healing took trust. Not in a romantic partner, but God. I latched it on to my treasures (money). I told God if I could build my trust with Him I knew my mate would be a cake walk. So I held Him at His word in Malachi 3:10 and I gave mine that I would give my tithe every pay no matter what, to show how much I wanted the healing of my trust issues.

I succeeded.

In that effort I learned that the next repair of my boat is to trust myself. As a marine mechanic on this one, sometimes I feel like I'm drowning. I decided to tether this one to my prayer life. The deeper my communication with Him the stronger my faith will be. Greater is He that lives in me...I can trust what's, or should I say who, is on the inside of me. This in turn allows me to trust me. To connect with the deeper since of self-awareness.

My prayer life is my North Star. As long as I listen for the still small voice, I can trust I have made the right decisions (and always have). The caveat is the more I learn to trust myself the more in love I fall with her as well. Which brings wholeness that will be appealing to my future spouse.

The voice passing in the night, just like The Theologian's Tale, is the Lover of my Soul.

OUT OF MY FAMILIAR

The healing process is still happening, there's still pain, still an itch you can't scratch, a limp, crutches and people signing off on all these things, but what's inside knows the true process of healing all that.

Are we (you) mistaking familiar with forever?

Initially I believed this only applied to romantic relationships.

Then God showed me that familiar is also your comfort zone.

Yea, that's what I said…

Comfort zones show up in many ways. At work, in relationships, even in something disguised as your diet. Eating the same meals day in and day out. What's really hidden is why.

Why is playing it safe in any of these areas more important than exploring outside your norm. Not just exploring but going after your true desires. Eating a food you never have but always wanted to try. Traveling abroad or giving someone a compliment to let them know you're interested.

What do we sacrifice for this comfort? The first thing I think of is peace of mind. Staying in a job that leaves you unfulfilled, continuing a romantic relationship because of the length of time, for the kids, or because the sex is good. Keeping up any activities because it's what you've always done? You can tell you're not really invested. You're just going through the motions. It comes natural, and you're good at it. What you want to be sure to do is not let good keep you from great.

Who do we let the familiar keep us from being? One of my familiar cycles was choosing the same guy in a different body. He is taller or shorter, lighter or darker, and on and on, but he is still emotionally unavailable. Insert abandonment and daddy issues here. My dad was for a long time emotionally unavailable. Also, for a long time I wouldn't let myself be vulnerable enough to find out why.

Ahh…yeah we think it's all on the other person to be what we need them to be. Even our parents. Not so. You won't get what you don't ask for. Even when you ask you may not get what you were expecting, but you do still get what you were asking for. An answer.

The healing process isn't comfortable. It's about answers that lead you to your truth or a new one. You see there's the pain of comfort as much as there is an ease in it. You hate your job, say you want more, but every day you do the bare minimum. More requires just that, more. Your romantic relationship has lost its fire, but you are waiting for and expecting your partner to light the flame again. You'd rather wait in your comfort of just having someone than speak up or rock the boat in fear they may leave.

What we truly desire is right outside what we know as familiar. The kid in us all is the one who holds the desired unquenchable truth of what we need and who we really want to show up as in the world. The healing is tending to that pain. Face it. The itch is soothed exploring something adventurous. Toss those crutches and work that limp by eliminating the excuses. The people that were signing off on you staying stuck or beside them on a low vibration may need to see you come up so they know it's ok for them to as well. Your healing may be the catalyst for their shift out of their comfort zones.

COPING

Just because you're not angry doesn't mean you don't need to heal.

Your joy may be expanding because you let someone help you manage the wound.

Anger is not the only symptom of pain. You can let the residue of the past plague you for years. It shows up as indecisiveness, people pleasing, self-sabotage, substance abuse, and physical abuse.

It could even show up as having the time of your life. Hence substance abuse. Yes, partying, splurging on items and experiences that are meaningless to dull the sting of whatever event has us in avoidance. It is one of the first things we do when we're hurting. How many times have you heard, "I just can't deal with this right now?" I believe no one should tell anyone how to grieve. Respectfully, no one knows how they would go through a traumatic event until they are in it. Eventually, though, we need to address our discomfort before it consumes us.

Before my biological mom was killed in 2001, there's no way you could've convinced me that I'd be cool, calm, and collected the night I drove from St. John's hospital in Detroit after identifying her body. I still get emotional just thinking about it, but in that moment, God truly took over. On that drive He told me He had me and

I was gonna be ok. He is still keeping that promise 20 years later.

Your grief may not be the loss of a loved one. It could be your income, your home, or even a sense of belonging. No matter what it is, we have all had a time we were coping with something.

Coping and numbing are not the same. Numbing is a form of coping in my non-medical opinion. Numbing is ignoring the pain. Coping is developing the skills to live through it. Grief, no matter the catalyst, is always waiting in the wings. It never leaves us. We just learn how to cope with it, or we numb it.

Forgiveness is a tool in the coping toolbox. Forgiving allows you to start the healing process. Letting go doesn't make you wrong and them right or that what happened to you was ok. It just states that you no longer will let this moment have power over the rest of your life. It signifies that you are ready for peace. Not letting bitterness set in and ruin or blur your opportunity for clarity is a great way to see yourself on the other side of the pain.

If you're anything like me, faith and prayer are in your toolbox as well. I'd have to say those are my best tools for coping with the challenges life and grief bring my way. I wouldn't have made it to forgiveness without prayer. To trust in prayer that your comfort and healing will come takes faith. They're my dynamic duo. It's funny how they are both weapons and tools. Like a hammer. Depending on how you use them, you can build or destroy.

I'll share one more thing that has made living and evolving from trauma a sanity saver…JOY! That's right joy. The positive choice to live in a continual state of joy. Please don't mistake this for toxic positivity. Joy is a choice. It takes effort to choose the joy you seek DAILY. This joy requires gratitude, grace, and self-awareness. When we are grateful it fills us up from the abundance God has provided in our lives. It reminds us this moment may be bad, but it too shall pass. That God has given us moments of bliss and we will experience several more as we go on living from today.

Giving ourselves grace in the moment allows us to look again. Look at the positive things that this experience has offered us or waiting for us on the other side of this pain.

Most of all, self-awareness lets us feel the feelings.

Yep, just sit with the feelings. Then decide how we will move forward. In our time and in our own way. When the betrayal has been self-inflicted, we may need even more time to see what choices we will and won't make next time.

See, we don't always see all the things plaguing us or holding us back until we're triggered. That's how I discovered some of my wounds still leaking all over my life. I wasn't angry anymore and had actually forgiven myself and those involved in most of my painful life experiences, but I hadn't really addressed the debris from the fallout of coping. My newfound insecurities, shame, and self-doubt that arose from actions, or the lack thereof, on my part hindered me from bringing my whole self into the room and heal beyond the freedom of forgiveness.

Once the grieving has subsided, we do the work of healing.

Whether that's self-examination or with a therapist. We have to do the work to recover.

For example: You get into a physical fight. This may be with someone you care about or not. You decide the details of this hypothetical scenario. A few days have passed, and you both apologize. All is forgiven. However, your black eye and their broken nose still have to heal. That takes medicine and time. Things have to be done to repair the damage the fight caused.

See what I mean? OK cool.

Now I know forgiveness is not always mutual, however this is the visual I wanted to share so take what you will from it.

Look at the underlying things happening in your heart and life that may be forgiven but not yet healed. In this effort you will go from coping in survival mode to thriving.

CIRCLE OF EVENTS

6th grade honor roll student called to the office
For after this day life as I knew it would never be the
    same
At the school's entrance sat a state car
My brothers inside
2 of the 3 I knew so far
My worse fear had come true
I already knew what they had come to do
In the principal's office they ran me their game
Using my mother's name while making me feel shame
As I approached the car
My brothers smiled
Delight filled their face
Not knowing tonight we all would live at a separate
    new place
The excruciating pain rang in my ears
As the parking structure echoed my brother's cries I did
    my best to wipe their tears
As each car went in a different direction
I thought
Now who will be their protection?
Mommy...they didn't even let us say goodbye
Here I sit tonight to cry
Askin'
Why God why?
Ripped from my family and put in a new one in the
    middle of the night
Whose idea was this?
They have to know this isn't right
Yeah heroin coursed through her veins
But this couple has a son who is mentally insane

I know she does drugs
But she gives the best hugs
When she O-Ded yes it was scary (sca-ree)
But I know she still loves...me
Male and female ex-foster kids they came to stay
Hmm he's 18 and he wants to play
Cute to me is what he said
This time he spent the night he slept in my bed
Almost 13 innocent I was
Until in my ear he whispered about his love
Now foster home number two
Back with my lil brothers yeah that's cool
I couldn't wait for the hugs and to give them each a kiss
Shortly after
I was informed
This is not a family this is a business
Physical, verbal, and emotional abuse was the weapon
    of choice

To kill our dreams and silence our voice
Once again like Tamar I had a brother...
Who wanted to be my lover
Good grades and a track star
Coaches across the country said I would go far
But not if her approval was my car
Daily it was made clear I was destined to be the statistic
You know the image of my mother
The dope fiend chick
17...pregnant...
Yeah you can keep this baby
Just let me see how much more the state will pay me
19 and the queen of this castle of torment was dead and
    gone
I was on the road of being on my own
Mommy...clean
Lovin' life
And...pretty (pret-te)
She was back
And still receiving love from me

THE SIDE YOU DON'T SEE

I got dressed for school, kissed my mama and said see you later. I was attending Remus Robinson Middle School. It was sixth grade. On this day I'm in class and I get called to the principal's office. Even my teacher was surprised and over the PA she inquired, "May I ask why?" Of course, they didn't share. Walking down to the office, I looked out the window and saw my two little brothers sitting in the state car. I was told we were leaving with a social worker.

We arrived at what was back then 801 Baltimore, here in Detroit. I guess it was where you transitioned from emergency placement to your foster home.

After hours of fear, waiting to see what was next. They came to let us know we would be leaving now. Unbeknownst to us we would be leaving in three separate vehicles. I remember hearing the screams from my brothers echoing through the parking structure. I felt so helpless. I have been taking care of them for so long. Who would do that now? Where are they going? Who will they live with? Most of all, when would I see them again?

I was driven to my first foster home. I kissed my mom goodbye in the morning and that night I lived with total strangers.

I didn't know it at the time, but the trauma after placement wasn't ever addressed. If you didn't act out, exhibit poor behavior or mental and emotional strain, you were fine. No need to ask if I needed someone to speak to about how this traumatic event impacted me. A child with no options. A child wondering and hoping to see their mother and brothers again. Afraid of what my life now and will look like.

The "new" family... The "mother" obese and on a cane. The "father" an abusive alcoholic, cursing his wife out, verbally abusing her daily. Was a better option than my Heroin addicted mother. Now, it is not lost on me, as an adult, that my mom being hooked on drugs was not safe or healthy either, but if the main goal was to place me in a home of my best interest, I'd say this was not a viable option either.

This wanna be wonderful home had its secrets, apparently kept from my social worker at the time. My new foster family had given me the impression that I was an only child, until the day they took me to the local mental institution to visit their son. Yes, a 12 year old girl who is trying to figure out how to manage this current pain, has to now navigate a psych ward to see someone she doesn't know, nor cares to.

To make matters worse, my new temporary parents brought my new brother home to live with us. He slept upstairs. Thank goodness. He was pretty cool until he, like his father, became intoxicated.

One day after school I was in the kitchen doing my homework. He was home with me. On this day his beverage of choice was straight vodka. He must have been drinking the entire day. He's screaming from the bathroom, "Help me! Little girl, you gotta help me!! by this time, I'm terrified as to how he may emerge from the bathroom. I grabbed a butcher knife to protect myself from the drunk man in my bathroom of whom I've been left home alone with. He yells again, little girl come in here, you gotta help me!" I pull away from the kitchen table and creep to the hallway and curl around the wall peeking into the bathroom to find my current adult step-brother has cut his stomach open from left to right. Blood running down onto his lap dripping into the toilet. I run from the hallway, panicked, and trying to dial 911. In a house covered in armor guard bars that in my state of fear I can't find a key, so I squeeze through the bars and run across the street to the neighbor's house. Even with the previously stated events, I was not removed from this home. Among several other inappropriate events I witnessed, I lost my virginity in this home to a former foster son my "new parents" would let visit from time to time. Someone who took advantage of my innocence.

Someone found my brothers. Yes, I was finally getting to see my two little guys again. The McCormicks, my current foster family, asked me how I felt about visiting them. I thought that was a strange question, but my answer was a resounding yes. After two visits, Mrs. Nelson talked my foster mother into letting me spend the night. I was elated. I arrived at the Nelson family's home and smiled at my brothers with such joy. We had a great night together. The next morning Mrs. Nelson asked me how would I like to live with my brothers? Well of course! At the time I probably said, "Yes ma'am."

The McCormicks were sad to see me go. I was going from being the very much younger child. Their son was 40+ years old. So, I was practically an only child. To moving in with the Nelson family. Mrs. Nelson had seven kids of her own, two of which still lived at home. I was now part of a family of ten.

Have you ever heard the saying, "You think you want something until you get it"? Well, that's what moving with this family and really missing my little brothers got me. Shortly after moving in, the honeymoon phase started to fade. One day Mrs. Nelson overheard us talking about family or being a family, and she leaned in and said, "This is not a family. This is a business."

No truer words had ever been spoken. She had family and friends she had recruited to become foster parents as well. She taught them all the tips and tricks on which kids bring in more money and why. Which leads to why we, me and my two brothers, were adopted. I'm sure way way way down deep she had a soft spot for us because she kept us around, but the main reason was so she could get more foster kids. After our adoption, every kid had some type of handicap, deformity, or mental illness. They brought in more money.

It was definitely business to her. I definitely didn't feel loved.

Speaking of her greed for more money. I believe it's the sole reason my oldest daughter is alive today.

To a degree, Mrs. Nelson was proud I had proven some of her snide remarks right. Trying to find love in all the wrong places and believing the poor tapes playing in my mind about what men and boys wanted from me. My junior year, I became pregnant. Her calling me a slut had manifested, at least in her mind. She took me to my prenatal appointments. Made sure she asked plenty of questions. What I believed to be her finally showing some concern for my life and/or needs was simply her buying time to see if my pregnancy as an adopted child would yield her more money in her monthly payment for me. By the time she found out the answer was no, it was too late for me to have an abortion.

Writing this makes me wonder if that's where my lack of trust comes from in all my relationships. Her showing she cared and then having the rug pulled out once I found out the truth. It's enough to make anyone suspicious.

EARTH, BRICKS, AND BOXES

You ever heard the song by Carole King and James Taylor, "I can make the earth move under my feet"? Great song! However, that lyric reminds me of a house we lived in on the west side of Detroit. The floor was so thin you could literally feel it move under your feet. Our house set off the alley. We were known as the house that had two front yards. They were divided by rose bushes. When I say we lived off the alley, I mean you opened the back door with caution and never at night unless you wanted to let rats in. It may not have been the sturdiest house, but I remember having a lot of fun there. I would dance to the Commodores song "Brick House." There wasn't a brick in sight on my body. I also loved anything by Diana Ross, with a T-shirt on my already long hair so it would be big like hers.

My brother and I thought jumping from our beds into a pile of clothes was way more fun than cleaning them up. Until the fun turned into the house almost burning down because my brother playing with a lighter set those very clothes on fire. Let's just say my mama showed us how our butts could burn as well after that.

Another memorable moment in this home that stuck with me, and I believe influences how I live today, is a special Christmas. if you've ever been the kid in class praying you have something to talk about or show off when Christmas break is over, then you know that pit in your stomach when your worst nightmare comes true. There's nothing under the tree on Christmas Eve. Yep, no gifts. It was getting closer to bedtime, and I was convincing myself something would be there when I woke up. I'm not sure if this was Christmas Eve or Christmas Day, but there was a knock at the door late in the evening. When the door opened, there was my favorite teacher and two other ladies with boxes. Huge boxes. My brother had trucks, army men, and blocks to learn with. Me, well, I couldn't stop smiling and crying. I got the one thing I wanted, the kitchen with all the food so I could play store and cook. Then I opened the paper and pencil sets. There were two dolls and clothes for me and my brother. I looked up at my teacher and smiled so wide. I did my best not to cry. I was so happy. The ladies that accompanied her were strangers, but I felt their hearts just the same. We thanked them all, and as my teacher waved goodbye, I knew someone other than my mommy would take care of me no matter what.

SELF

Don't let us be so selfless that we do less for ourselves. Giving is its own reward, when done with the right motives. Most givers are so excited about the recipient's reaction they never consider the depletion from their own energy or life.

I am now adopting the same motto for my self-preservation bank as I've done for my closet and dresser. In my wardrobe, the rule is: if an item comes in, one has to go out. For my self-preservation I say: if something is shared, I have to replenish. It reminds me that I have to give myself at least as much love as I give others, if not more.

I don't know about you, but I love a great view. So I thought of this as a waterfall. Waterfalls are beautiful. A waterfall pours ferociously. It is only from the flow of the river or the melting iceberg that the downpour is plentiful. The view may still be awe-inspiring without the water, but the more water flow, the more exquisite the visual. It's the same with giving.

You continue to fill your cup so the overflow is healthy and expansive. All that flows from you is life-giving and not draining. You don't end up resenting your efforts or the recipient. Giving with this premise becomes exhilarating because you're looking for the next opportunity to share, while looking forward to the time you get to restore yourself.

This is not a free pass to be selfish. By no means are we to be self-indulgent only. This serves no one. Nope, not even ourselves. Taking care of yourself is never selfish. By doing so you're already ahead of the game to take care of others. My oldest daughter's Big Mama taught me years ago that I couldn't take care of my kids if I didn't take care of myself. There's no one more important than my children. I want to give them the best version of me at all times. When I diminish my personal resources without taking time to restore my mental well-being I can get grumpy, lack focus, make poor choices, or shrug responsibilities. This is not the way to build wealth, enjoy life, or value those I love and serve.

Most of the time, when selflessness is done with mindfulness for both parties, no one loses. It's all heartfelt and healthy.

HEROINE

My mommy was killed in 2001, June 2, 2001.

She died once before this. I was about 11 or 12 years old.

She had Od'ed (overdosed) on the couch from heroin.

I had to call 911 to save my mommy from herself.

What she couldn't do was save me from the testimony God had for me. This one I'm sharing with you today.

Our neighbors downstairs helped me and my brothers until the paramedics got there.

My mommy needed a few second chances, and God was gracious enough to oblige.

I believe this day may have contributed to some other neighbors reporting my mother to DHS (DHHS). Which began me and my brothers' journey into foster care.

Now some would probably jump to resentment or blame, but I never felt that for my mommy. The depth of love I have for her never changed. I believe it was the open and honest relationship we always had that made my compassion overflow.

Bad choices don't always equal bad people.

Forgiveness is a way to reconcile and dispel regret. At least in this relationship dynamic.

My mom didn't get to live out my childhood with experiences of clarity, and that's ok. She had her moments with my kids and her other grandkids that I wouldn't trade for all the riches in the world. Heroin may have plagued a part of my story, but I'm the heroine in the end.

CLEARANCE JACK

You thought I would wait on you
Like a rain check
You thought you could return with your discounted
    love
Well, you missed the Target
I got smart
Like Kmart
I shut down
Like Walmart's
"Always low prices"
So were your standards
Fortunately for me
I've raised mine
Like taxes
It's guaranteed
No more games
I took a note from Toys R Us
Like Bergdorf
I want a good man
I had a little talk with Jesus
He opened His Foot Locker
And shared Victoria's Secrets
He said as women we need to use our Lids
Our love is Lush
Aromatic and cleansing

Navigating love can be an adventure
Like the Amazon
But always remember
we're Prime
Helzberg Diamonds ain't got nothing on far above
    rubies
One of a kind
like a gift from Merci Cadeaux
Like IKEA He helped me put it all together
I'm not returning to Play it Again Sports
Not visiting Priscilla's
But I am vibrating higher
Thanks to the ultimate
LensCrafters my Visionworks
I don't know if he's one of America's Best
But as long as he doesn't act Forever 21,
Focus less on God's World and more on God's word
I can handle the Low(es)
as long as he takes care of home
We'll be woven together like Joann's Fabric
Despite what Eve did with that Apple
You're just an ex, and like TJ I'm the Maxx. Are we
    clear?
Like Gucci
I'm done with you.

MISSING MOM

Some say grief comes while life is happening, but today
    I feel like life comes while grief is happening
You're trying to maneuver while not feeling
While not crying
While not processing
While not leaning into it
I miss her immensely
It's been with me for weeks
Her spirit
I've dreamt of her
Seen her
I feel her on some days
Her spirit
It's like a comfy weighted blanket
Today after church
It hit me
Grief
the tears
just like its presence
comes in waves
Today I'm crying
Today I'm sharing
Today I'm within
Today I only have enough me, for me
and I'm not sure if that's enough

Today there will be numbing
Today there will be avoidance
Today there will be isolation
Today there will be coping
and that's ok

THE 3 PEOPLE GOD LET INVADE
MY HEART

She's my firecracker and roadrunner. The Youngest.

He's my sounding board in all things creativity and business. The middle Man.

She's my reading buddy and the one that reels in my overthinking. The Eldest.

All of them are my equalizers. They balance me out.

Becoming a mother when you're a child yourself is a feat in and of itself. Managing pain, insecurity, fear and being riddled with unanswered questions. You grow up with your kids. You find yourself while God allows you to guide them.

My age 17 -1991 daughter's birth

My age 21 -1994 son's birth

My age 24 -1997 daughter's birth

I had my last kid before the age my mom had her first, which was 25, when she gave birth to me. Her only girl.

My mom was my best friend. I'm blessed to have as strong a bond with my three incredible children. I'm also grateful my kids got to experience my mommy's love as I did. She was an exceptional grandmother.

What's interesting is that I never wanted kids growing up. I wasn't dreaming of a wedding and 2.5 children. I'm sure my upbringing played a role in this line of thinking.

Now I wouldn't trade motherhood for anything in the world. To love three people equally, while loving them uniquely has been the most incredible experience God has allowed. What makes this even more fabulous is being loved the same way in return. I am grateful that my kids see me as their mother and a woman with her own dreams.

Some say my kids are my whole world. I know based on the way we love each other this is not true. I'll admit for a long time I believed it was. Our goals and ambitions are just as important to us all. My kids are the closest to me when it comes to family. With my mom in heaven and my dad and I building a love we hadn't shared while I was a kid. My children fill a place in my heart I don't share with anyone else. However, supporting each other through the ups and downs in our lives and family dynamic, I know we are not consumed with each other, but don't you dare try to come between us.

As a good mother doing her best to give them all the love, wisdom, and biblical principles they need to become value adding citizens of this world, I had to climb out of the whole I had put myself in as a mom. Remember, I said I had to change my thinking about them being my whole world. It was so easy to get lost in them. I was in the depth of childhood trauma when I became a mom. So, this unconditional love was like a salve to my wounds. When my son was born, I thought I had found love. That I would have a family. Unfortunately, it was another relationship gone south. But I was a mommy. Now to two beautiful babies and I was good at it. So, I just kept being a mommy. Long as they were good, I was good.

You don't know what you don't know. I was loving them under the guise of achievement and still hadn't healed the hurt that made me a mom in the first place. So, I chose another guy while wrapped in my trauma. I poured all I had into my kids because they loved me, and I loved them and nothing was breaking that bond. To this day, it's solid as rock. Their love was all I needed to get through anything.

My saying is "It's always been me and my three". Til the wheels fall off it will be this way.

Kids are mirrors. Reflections that talk. When they started pointing out things I stopped doing or ways I had stopped being that they believed brought me joy. I knew it was time to make a shift.

I had to take a honest look at my life and ask myself who was I now. As well as who did I want to be as a mom and more importantly as a woman.

I didn't want to get to the end of my life with regrets of dreams on the shelf I never pursued. I wanted to show my kids that they actually do come true if you have the audacity to step into what God has called you to do, be, and say. I had an assignment beyond their mom, and it was time to get to completing it.

My kids freed me from mom guilt. They encourage me to show up fully. What's even more awesome is they get in on my dreams as much as I am in theirs. They're my glam squad, street team, tech support, and so much more. I love how we are all multifaceted and our talents complement one another. Although I do believe my son got in the talent line about ten times more than should be humanly possible.

It brings me so much JOY to know I am free to be me while immersing myself in being their mommy.

WHAT'S IN HER NAME

Since the womb she has done things in her own timing.

The Cosby Show had just went off and I really wanted to watch more TV, but the pain in my stomach was too much. My stepmother came by my room and asked why I was in the bed so early. I was known for staying up late. I told her my stomach was hurting. She asked me where, I indicated the lower part of my stomach and felt like it was going around my back. She yelled, girl get up, you in labor.

We get in the car and head to the hospital. The more we drive the better I feel. We arrive at the hospital. I get hooked up to all the monitors. I'm back in pain. Yet, no dilation. So, they have me walk the hall. Not fun. I walk some more. No action. They send us back home. Once in the car again. No pain. This kid just wanted to go for a drive. To this day she loves to travel.

The next day I'm in more pain. Another trip to the hospital only confirms that she just loves to go for a ride. Hours have passed and now I have to be induced. Whenever I tell this story, or any about their births, it reminds me that God had a plan for their lives and developed their personalities before I knew them.

Her senior year of high school she decided to sport on the back of her senior jersey the word(name) "AU-

DACIOUS". It fits her to a T. She reminds me often that she gets it from me, but I still believe she has always been way more recklessly bold than I. It's one of the things I admire most about Sharla.

She is named after my mom. Sharlene. Well, she's also named for my dad. Her middle name is given for my dad as well. I missed my parents so much and I wanted parts of them and my birth name to be kept when she was born because at the time, I thought I had lost that part of me forever when I was put in foster care and then adopted. I'm grateful she got to meet them both and experience parts of her that she carries in her name.

When you're born you may get your mother's eyes or your dad's smile. Everyone looks forward to seeing who had the strongest genes. In our case one genetic connection Sharla's dad and I passed on was Sickle Cell Anemia Disease. A blood disease that is debilitating on a daily basis in a number of ways. The fact that she is a high achieving student and person that never used her disease as a crutch makes me so proud as her mother. Being raised by a teen mom, who has faced her own challenges and trauma, Sharla never let sympathy be a driving force to play small to. Those who fight with this disease are dubbed Sickle Cell Warriors. Sharla is truly living up to the name.

One thing we share is our love for books. We sometimes will have a reading race to see who will finish their book first. We've been doing it since she was a little girl. I'll admit it here, she usually wins. She's a forever student. Even when she's not in school she's a student of life.

I believe that's something else she gets from me, being a seeker.

Sharla loves to serve. Her non-profit "Sovereign Gift" helps her stay connected with the community and feeds her eager heart for learning more about the world. As much as she is a seeker, she is one of my greatest teachers.

THE BEAUTY OF MY BABY

It's funny that my youngest is the old soul of my three children. The way she cooks, the music she loves, how she wraps herself in a blanket with a cup of coffee and watches television. I nick named her granny because she's an old lady in a youthful body.

Her name is Alantis. She is named after her dads favorite Isley Brothers song "Voyage to Atlantis". We compromised on not having the first "T" (Atlantis) I wasn't having it. I let him have the first name and I chose the middle name. Her first name really fits her. She goes with the flow til you make her turn cold towards you.

It baffles me how big her heart is but she's not affectionate at all. I steal my hugs anyway. She is an encourager. She will support her friends. As well as share with the homeless. Just don't get mushy cause she's not for it.

She's the baby of my three. She's her dad's only child (as I'm writing this). She was the only grandchild on his side until age 7 I believe. The only girl in the family on his side as well. Her father's parents had all boys. So, to say she was spoiled is an understatement. She could do no wrong in any of her grandparents' eyes.

When things went left for me and her dad as a couple it took my baby on a spiral well into her teenage years. Finding yourself while losing a major part of who is supposed to help shape you, brings its own set of challenges.

She took me down through there as a parent. I never let go though. Loved ones closest to you tend to get the brunt of your pain until healing comes. I didn't always have the answers. We grew together navigating emotions we both needed to process. It made our bond stronger.

One way I connected with my babies when I was pregnant was putting headphones on my belly with my favorite music playing. I believe this attributes to their exceptional taste in music. I don't have any scientific proof but let me have this. LOL. Any of my kids can have the aux cord when we have jam sessions. However, when it comes to watching a movie or TV, call Alantis. She is so fun to watch anything with. You believe she knows each character personally.

She's rooting for people, even though it's not a competition. You'll hear her yelling at people and asking why are they being stupid as if they owe her money. She is completely invested in every storyline, and she reels me in every time.

One of my favorite moments we shared is when we were on a car ride and she said, "Mommy I use to be so upset watching you pray and praise God the way you do when we were homeless or just going through a tough time. I was like, why does she believe in that stuff and we out here struggling. Then I started praying. Once I had my own relationship with God, I understood it. You trust Him and just when you need Him He shows up. I get it now. I get it now. That's what you were teaching us. To have our own thing with God. He showed me. I really get it now." I was so proud. Yes, I cried. Don't judge me. To know how your baby was hurting at one time in her life, and to always pray that you're being the example you believe God desires for you to be, then to know that the seeds are blooming in her heart, mind and soul was such a blessing to hear in her own words. Not because I'm so great, but because God is so remarkably good.

It's like the line from the poem Sermons We See "I'd rather see a sermon than hear one any day; I'd rather one should walk with me than merely tell the way." I've always told my kids I don't have a heaven or hell to put you in. The relationship you have with Jesus is all your own.

My prayers may protect you, but it's your communication with God that will shape your life. It's a blessing to watch that manifest.

How I show up on set at times is all in her hands. She is my glam squad leader. She does my make-up and colors my hair. Well, she had to teach me how to color my own hair since she decided to move to California. She's my beauty guru.

All my kids have a boldness I admire. They all say they get it all from me. Boldness, sarcasm, strength and sense of humor. I stand in awe of them often. They are unapologetically themselves. It has taken me some time to work my way to that. I still have a ways to go.

Alantis is our watch dog. Don't let your eyes linger too long when we're out in any combination. She's gonna ask how we can help you. She's fearless and feisty.

Just as glamorous as she gets on a daily basis, she brings even more beauty to my life every day.

CENTER STAGE

To be the middle child he towers over his sisters. At a pinnacle of 6 feet 6 inches, even if he wasn't an incredible kid, we'd be looking up to him.

He calls us his girls. He's our protector for sure.

He's an observer.

A kid of few words until he's writing. Yes, songs or script writing, he's got it honest. My first love is writing. He also has another famous author in his blood line on his dad's side. He is so talented all on his own. I don't even know where to start. Writer, musician, artist, choreographer, digital creator, producer, fashion icon, who happens to own his own record label. Like I stated before, I believe he got in the talent line several times before he left heaven.

Our bond sure comes out of the creativity we both are filled with. We see the world in such similar ways. We can talk for hours about projects we're working on, music we love, building businesses, and so much more.

Our birthdays are exactly three weeks apart. I love when we get to do something just our own during that month. It's usually a really cool movie or documentary he wants to share only with me.

I also love how we hang out and critique new music of favorite artists. Corey is a researcher like me. His favorite artist is Beyonce' and I always tease him saying he knows things about her even Jay Z doesn't know. I mean people who have been on her team for years follow my son on social media. That's pretty close.

Corey was named after his father's bestfriend. I love that his name means Gods peace. He is that mild mannered and is usually the settler of disputes. He is the sound judgement for a lot of his friends. He is constantly making sure I'm good. I'm in awe of the love he has for me.

One of our unique moments shared was a regular mom and son chat about life and faith. He stood in my bedroom doorway and said, mom if you don't get in heaven ain't nobody getting in. The way I cried. Listen. Even as adults they are watching and listening. I believe God sends moments like this to remind us of the path we are to remain on. Perhaps to reel us back in if we start to stray or to lean in even when it gets tough.

Corey has a boldness all his own while remaining true to his meekness. Let's be clear, please don't misunderstand that as weakness. He will get you together real quick. I guess it's pretty clear we ain't to be played with.

My mother and Corey had a bond that was undeniable. I won't call him her favorite because she spoiled them all in her own way. What I will say is that I don't think Corey's birthday being the last time we saw my mom alive is a coincidence. She was killed two days later. The day before her birthday. Yes, the closeness is irrefutable.

He's the middle child who's a big deal. Every mother believes their kids are fantastic beings. One thing I love about Corey is he is a star in his own eyes. He doesn't need me or anyone else to tell him who he is or who he'll become. In this regard I am a huge fan.

WORTHY ALONE

I will never be without love as long as I have it for myself.

MEN-DING

Today I called my dad to tell him I was having a rough time. I usually cheer up when I call him, so I did. It made both of our days.

I had never heard my dad talk about God the way he did. I don't remember him talking about Him at all. He was so encouraging and nurturing. Confirming what I already know about God to be true. It felt amazing. It was just how the talks would go with my mom.

Him telling me God knew my heart, I'm gonna be ok, I'm human. Bad things happen to good people sometimes, but I will be ok because God knows what I need, and He doesn't lie. It just warms my heart to keep having these moments with my dad. The healing is the breaking of chains. The curse of poor relationships with fathers in my family is broken.

Healing in and of relationships period.

HIDE AND SEEK

I was waiting for permission from a ghost
Of which I never needed when they were alive
I was never gonna get their yes
My power then was greater than they'd seen in their
     lifetime
And it hindered them from letting the child, me, be all
     they could never be
The mirror was too painful

So they inflicted the harshness on me and anyone that
     reminded them of me
With each hit, whether from hand or word
They knew I'd hide
That gave them great pride
Because they believed they had broke my stride
Hoping I'd retreat further inside
But with every day I'd rise
Speak to my inner guide
Find a way to continue
Even while I cried

ONE WORD FROM GOD

One woman (my stepmom) had me at the mercy of her words. Now I know I have only one person's words to live by — God's!

What God says about me challenges the lies I've believed that were spoken to me or developed from my life experiences. When I find myself in God's word, it is so liberating. Which in turn makes more of His word come alive to me. Scriptures like Romans 12:2 "…renewing of your mind…" because this is exactly what's happening. Being told daily, in so many words, that you don't matter and won't amount to anything starts to stick. It drives the message home, especially when everyone is making decisions for you, except the ones you're wishing would happen. It solidifies your deepest fears that they are in fact right.

The fact that I am in my right mind after molestation, rape, watching my mom be physically abused by her boyfriend and me hiding under the bed, looking at a shotgun wondering if I had the strength to use it so I could save her, my mom's substance abuse, believing I would never see her again, my step mom's physical abuse bestowed on me and my brothers at times just because we were breathing, and so many other things you'll read about in these pages lets me know that His word spoken to and read by me is the word I need to believe and judge my life by.

No one knows the vision God has for their life except as He reveals it to them. Your circumstances, age, race, or gender don't matter. He loves us. Period. That's all. Even when life makes you feel completely alone, He is there.

Your testimony and tenacity are what someone else is waiting to see and hear. For so long all I could hear, even long after her death, was all the negative dialogue she recited to me. Slowly, over time, I finally let the power of God's word drown out my stepmom's crippling annotations about who I could become. I'm so thankful for my courage to float above her projected pain.

Using your voice is another way to deafen the sounds of all the negative influences that have impacted your self-esteem. There's no rule that says you can't help and heal at the same time. Conquering your trauma serves you and the world on a level only God can promote you to. Listening to His voice as your guide is key. The only word you really need is "TRUST" in Him.

Romans 12:2
And be not conformed to this world:
but be ye transformed by the renewing of
your mind, that ye may prove what is that good,
and acceptable, and perfect, will of God.

WITHIN

Self-exploration is such a beautiful experience
Your hands should be the first to hold your heart
If we did as much work on it, as we do on the outside
There'd be no hang-ups that make us wanna hide

DIMINISHED

How long will you compromise your peace for someone else's comfort?

Sometimes the good thing is not a God thing. When we think of God's will for our lives, we think about right and wrong, good and evil. If it falls in the right or good category, we believe God approves. If it is not our assigned calling in that season, it's all bad.

Yes, this means taking promotions at work, helping family members, loaning a friend money, etc. All good things are not our assignments.

This may be the breeding ground for resentment or your own missed blessings.

This poor stewardship of our time, talent and resources will cause us to misplace blame when frustration (aka resentment) sets in because our motives may be skewed and not aligned with the will of God.

By no means am I saying giving is wrong or climbing the corporate ladder. When done at the wrong time it can be a hinderance. There are lessons that God wants our loved ones to learn in real time. As well as your next level looking like remaining on the rung, you're on with greater impact.

We can love on others to a fault, never checking our capacity to extend the offer of support. Then losing faith when the cost of our peace becomes too expensive.

The ROI we're looking for is changed behavior. The fruit of healing and growth. What we are failing to realize is in some cases the one who has the capacity to bring lasting change in our loved ones life is God and what we in fact are providing is just temporary relief of the symptoms created by a much deeper wound. Their unhealed pain ends up infecting areas of our lives in subtle ways, but still depleting us.

Distractions are not always presented as "bad" things so being vigilant to seek God before we move or continue to serve in the way we have in the past will give us the discernment we need to be more effective in our relationships.

REMNANTS

My book editing today includes this very thing:

I have been living & loving myself from the residue of me I have left after serving everyone else. In turn I was teaching others how to treat me, as well as putting out the energy that scraps or less than, is what I believed I deserved. A subconscious belief that I didn't need as much as I gave...

NOTE/POEM TO MYSELF

I have given so much of myself and heart away I don't
    have anything left for me.
I am on a path to fill myself back up
I don't want to give away more than I feed myself
My needs matter!
My heart matter!
I matter!
I love you Niccole
#thatisall

GUT-WRENCHED

I'm not gonna ignore my gut,
but I'm not gonna talk myself
out of love anymore.

DADDY ISSUES

Today these words "Father" "Daddy" and their definitions have come full circle.

The thoughts of the fact that I've dated, even up until this day, men who are hardly around. How my dad was. He never committed to my mom, and no real true commitment has ever been given to me.

The word of the day from Joel Osteen asked, "Who's your daddy?"

Tonight, watching PBS Wayne Dyer's daughters sing and read about him being a dad.

During this show, I realized again that my life — childhood has shown up in my adult life in ways I hadn't noticed before

None of my children's fathers are committed to a woman or in their lives at the time of writing this.

Amen.

*When there is an unexplainable depth of pain in your life it is not necessarily the situation or events that are having you experience the sorrow, but God digging up the root of the moments that are hindering your prog-

ress to be and experience God's best.*

SPADES

"It's not the cards you're dealt, but how you play the hand." This quote by Randy Pausch was like a mantra or motto of sorts for me, until now. As you've been reading, you can see my hand pretty much sucked. I once believed my drive and resilience were all that I had pushing past the limits my childhood offered. Then I realized it wasn't Blackjack or Poker I was playing. It was more like a good game of Spades. Now you know if you've ever played Spades, it's a team effort. Your teammate is called your partner. You want them to be skilled, obviously. More important, you want them to pick up where you're lacking, if need be. This is how I see my hand I've been dealt. My hand is a 1 and a possible. For those who have never played, that's how many books I can make with the cards I'm holding. My partner, however, has been dealt a killer hand. With their hand, my 1 and a possible has become a BOSTON! My partner, you ask. Oh, that's God! He took my 1 and a possible and cleaned up on our opponents. We haven't got up from the table yet. Without Him, like in Blackjack or Poker, I would've folded a long time ago.

WITNESS

I was about seven years old. This house we were at was very dark. Now, I'm not sure if I'm remembering the house or the energy, but I do remember the floors and the things I saw.

My aunt was tied to a chair, and he was walking in front of her very displeased. Then WHAM! The pistol struck her face. Blood flew across the wall like sputtered ketchup out of a bottle. No matter what she said, he was not letting up. I don't remember exactly what the issue even was, but based on the events of my childhood, I'm sure drugs or money were involved. Oddly, as I'm playing this back now to write this, I can't say I was terrified or even frightened at the time. I'm sure I was, but I don't remember it that way. I just know I watched her take on this pain, abuse, and blame like a champ. Maybe I don't remember being scared because these types of moments were commonplace. I'm not sure. Maybe this became a learned behavior for me as an adult because of this moment. Just stuff it down and bear it. Endure, it'll be over soon. I wasn't beaten physically by any man, but once in a good while my stepmother knew just how to hit and hurt me in ways that left a scar both mentally and physically at times.

I remember years later telling my aunt that I remembered this unfortunate event in her life. She was stunned.

Her face in shock. Do you, she asked. Yes I do, auntie. Then, as stated above, I went into detail about that time. She said, you were so young, how did you remember that? I told her that it's been with me forever. That's not something you forget.

I'm sharing this, not just as something to show you, my reader, that I've lived through a lot. I'm also sharing to tell parents, aunts, uncles, and the like, think of kids as little sponges around your feet. Then picture your life spilling all over the floor. They are absorbing it all. Every move you make. Every event in your life you expose them to will be a part of their story as well. Allow them to soak up something they won't want to blot out later.

Now, I'm not sure if this incident was the same day or not, but it's how I see it in my mind. Whenever I think or talk about my aunt being pistol-whipped, I see this next incident as well. Like it's in the same house, just in a different room.

My mom and her friends would get high together most times because my mom was what you'd call the plug. She never had to beg, borrow, or steal for drugs. She knew who had the good stuff and would get them to it, so they would most times pay for her hit too.

On this day, apparently a friend got a little too heavy handed and went into a seizure. I heard a thud and a lot of yelling, frantic voices. My mom screaming get a spoon, hurry up and get me a spoon! I ran to the kitchen grabbed the spoon and handed it to my mom. She said, I have to pull his tongue down! He can't swallow his tongue. She yelled to a friend, hold his head still so I can open his mouth. She got the spoon in and got him calmed down. All I remember is the fear in the room and no one calling for emergency assistance. The things we'll learn, to keep doing the things we want to do even if they're not good for us.

CHOICES

The home we lived in when we were taken from my mom was somewhere and/or something that also wasn't good for my mom. We lived in a two-family flat on the east side of Detroit. It's funny when people ask what side of Detroit I am from, but I always say both. I lived a little bit of everywhere, on both sides.

Back to the bad choice to live in this two-story den of deception. We lived in the upstairs flat. My mommy, brothers, and I. Downstairs, a husband and wife. I don't remember them having kids. The wife was a chocolate brown lady. Her feet were also brown, and I don't mean the top. She wasn't well-kept like my mommy loved to be. You couldn't get in any bed with a dirty body, let alone dirty feet, in my mama's house.

One day, as my brothers and I played in the back bedroom, we heard a loud noise downstairs. My mom ran in the room and said, "Stay in here." We hid in the closet. The noises got closer. The police swung the closet door open. We looked up terrified. They told us it was ok, and we could come out. Our flat was trashed. Furniture flipped, cabinets emptied, and mommy standing there with pain on her face. It was probably shame now that I think about it. The lady and her husband were drug dealers so our house got raided too.

SOMEONE TO LOVE

They met as children
Spent and enormous amount of time together
They enjoyed dirt bikes and gravel spin outs at the
    school playground
See, she was a tom boy
As time went on
Their friendship saw her through pain that other than
    God
No one could console
As she endured the hurt
Their friendship withstood the storms
She begun to trust this friend more and more
The secrets they held along with pain and laughter
Began a journey into learning to like what they saw in
    each other
Good and bad
The more time they spent alone
The stronger their bond became
Late nights up together
Dates spent reviewing ideas, hopes, and dreams
She found herself falling in love
Asking could this be possible
Someone who knew her faults; flaws; and mental,
    physical, and emotional battle scars
Could love her
Could truly love her
She would pray at night

And ask God to make her the woman this friend
Needed her to be
Help her to withstand the chaos
That would come their way
And to enjoy the pleasantries of life
Along the road to destiny
The closer they got
The stronger their bond became
When she looked in the mirror
She blushed from the thoughts of their union
At times she would laugh out loud
At the silly things they did together
This relationship developed her character,
Shaped her views, and strengthened her values
Her confidence and courage
Grew from the compliments and encouraging pep talks
This friend would give
Through the hurt and heartbreak of the men that came
To detour their friendship never destroyed their love
It actually fueled the fire
And increased the flame
That made this love stronger
She came raw and uncut to this friend
She asked if they were up for the challenge
To conquer their fears about this love
And venture off into the things
That brought them the most pleasure
As this friend held her head and heart
They leaped with her into her passion
She knew she had found the one
Yes this someone to love
Was her
And she is me

IMAGES

I want to make a collage
Of our mistakes
So we can reminisce
About how we loved each other through them
As you rest I want to peek into
Your dreams
Travel to the future and take a snapshot
Of your destiny
I'd like to drape myself
In the most delicate fabric

And dance in the picture
That your words paint of me
In my inhibitions I want you to capture
All your favorite parts of me
I want to go back in time
And get each of our sonograms
For at inception
Was our romance designed
Daily I'll send you photographs
Of the sunrise
To remind you
My love is limitless
Some say image is everything
As long as
Views, values, and commitment
Stay in focus
We will look good
In any light

HEAD PSA

He tried to give you the world
But that was never enough
You always wanted your home girl's stuff
He wined and dined you
With nights out on the town
But all you could do
Was put a brother down
He took you on trips across the country
But all you did
Was talk about how his boy had more money
He got a college degree
But you told him
That ain't shit
You'll always be beneath me
She came one day and set by his side
Listened to his pain
And took it all in stride
She liked his courage
And didn't bruise his pride
But you were the one he wanted for his bride
You kept saying what you would and wouldn't do
Ugh that's nasty who do I look like to you?
She listened to his problems
Some you caused and others you didn't
He started to smile more

I think the brotha was smitten
He started to come home
And clutch his phone
Some nights he slept on the couch
While you lie in bed alone
I would be remiss
If I failed to mention
These two friends one day
Decided to kiss
They knew two wrongs didn't make a right
But when apart
They thought about each other all night
His head was clouded
He told his friend
I think we should slow this down
If not bring it to an end
She said fine
I knew you came with limitations
But it's cool I have no expectations
For a while they went on as to have never met
He did think about her from time to time
She had a smile he could never forget
He asked you again if you would please him in that way
It's only oral sex
It won't cause any pain
But again you looked at him
And said nigga you must be insane
Who knew on this day
Curiosity
Would get the best of him
See, he ran into the good friend at the gym

After a little chit chat
They decided on a plan to meet
It would be a risk but oh so sweet
The pleasure he sought came without all that beggin'
    and pleading
She gave him just what was needing
As she drove home
She was thinking
Damn his unborn was yummy
And now you wondering why he walking in lookin' at
    you funny
See I don't condone cheating
But the next time it's yo man you thinking about
    mistreating
Don't be surprised
When you find out he's creepin'

CHEMISTRY

Just the fact that you are in the same room with me is
    enticing
The injections of your testosterone in my atmosphere
Makes me feel as if I'm experiencing some type of
    chemical imbalance
When I left my pheromones to permeate your presence
The signature of my scent had your head spin 360
    degrees
In search of the stimuli

The distance between us did not stop the tones from the
    vibration of your voice box
From infusing my ear drums with a longing for
    whispers of pillow talk
As you worked the room and made your way closer to
    me
I could feel my body temperature rise
In your embrace what was intended to be a friendly
    hello
Became an invitation to a pleasure filled destiny
Upon our exit of the party
We drove off in the vehicle of anticipated inoculation of
    bliss
The craving for an intravenous hit of your love drug
Made my body perspire and tremble
Eager for the moment you would lay me down
And examine every inch of my anatomy
Arriving at the appointed place

We entered eager to be cured of the physical anguish
Endured as we had traveled
As we disrobed the genetics of our family trees
Were gazed upon in delight
Succumb to the essence of one another
We surrendered to the therapeutic tactile elements
As our fingerprints left hints of exotic sensations along
    each other's epidermis
With your lips traces of your DNA were left on my
    pores
Down my back
Around to my navel
Back up to my lips
I gripped your masculine edifice
As you spread my legs to explore the purest of my
    femininity
The dew of my nectar covered your blood gorged male
    organ
As my thighs met your waist and my legs extended
    across your back
Our bodies began to thrust
My breast became palatable to your tongue
And as if I was the one consuming a mother's natural
    nutrition
I became full with a hunger for an orgasmic release
Reflexes and muscular contractions
Created by the friction that ignited a flame
Only to be doused by the chemicals leaving each of us
Our bodies exploded with a chemical reaction
That displayed signs of euphoria and fatigue

DISTANT LOVER

Through the stained-glass window of your soul
You see an image of a shell of the love you once knew
It's dressed in the evidence of purity that once was
I want more than anything to invite you in
But the constant of my reality
Plagued by choices that should
Have only been in fiction
Keep me distant
I keep you at bay
For fear that not only our love
But you as well may be destroyed
My heart wants what my world
Cannot afford
The mate you would be
Does not deserve the darkness
Of my soul
For the windows I peer through
Are of a murky resolution
And the image you see
To me
Displays a shattered reflection
I too believe our love would
Be intense and the energy
Well spent
I know you were sent to me by

Angels from above
Only someone that close to God
Could create such love
No matter the intent of my heart
My previously traveled trails
would have you spiral into an
Unforeseen wonderland to be
Consumed by unimaginable images
That would destroy your delicate beauty
How I loved that you didn't hold me to lofty
    expectations
And drenched me in admirable affection
But still I must depart
For it is only for your protection

LACK-A-DOODLE-DO

Is lack born out of feelings of not being enough?

Is lack manifested from our insecurities?

Doubt, fear, uncertainty, and perhaps even grief due to loss that we hold like a badge of honor instead of feeling and releasing until the next wave

Due to poor mindset life is mundane and the only excitement is the next circumstance we should've or could've avoided

We say we don't want this life, but continue to create or manifest the exact outcome we stay up at night praying to avoid

Most know that what you focus on grows. Yet we continue to let that negative thought drive us. I'm going to do "XYZ" to change "ABC." Instead our focus should be I'm doing "XYZ" to change the lives of foster children all over the world or I'm creating "XYZ" to enhance the lives of mothers who need a little time back in their schedule.

These types of thoughts change the energy emitted therefore shifting the energy returned back to you

The above thoughts are from a place of abundance

What you have is what you're giving, not lacking, so lack is no longer an option by which you operate, so growth, prosperity, and joy are increased

It goes back to intention. Asking yourself why you're

doing something. What's your motivation, not just the desired outcome, but why.

The rent is due. The kids' tuition is due. I need gas money. Those are valid needs, but still from a place of lack.

I'm lacking rent money so I'm going to do "XYZ."

The kids tuition is going up. I need to change "ABC" more this year, still lack.

The rent is always due, preparation meeting opportunity is favor and I'm motivated by the lives I'll change, the strength and discipline I've developed to help others. Abundance mindset, the rent still gets paid, but with a renewed mindset and since it's from a place of abundance there will be overflow and God promises more than enough.

Lack and scarcity are eliminated with positive mental shifts. Removing this thought pattern frees you to explore possibilities for resources that become solutions.

LOVE OF THE BROKEN

Your spirit broken before you knew it existed
How could you know honestly when you were born in
    a lie ridiculed for your very existence
How could your quest for love be persistent
Empty promises left you void of emotion
Now gone
Your only dream to be alone or better yet so long
Suicide your ticket to better dead than wrong

For just once you'd like a place for your heart to hide
    someone to stroke or boost your pride
Nothing like those who made you their pleasure in dark
    places
Even your daydreams couldn't help you forget their
    faces
This couldn't be what the good book meant by love
    each other the same
Because what mommies and daddies did caused you
    pain
Relationship
honesty
commitment
trust
That doesn't happen for people like us
Love is not an option when all you've been taught is lust
The web of deception left you feeling a sense of

imperfection
looking for love with no guidance
Or direction
you found sex and took it as affection
Open now are your eyes with a couple more bruises to
your pride
To avoid the hurt you're mindful now about who you
let see your sensual side
You can talk about how your past makes you feel
It's a difficult journey as you heal
But so worth it because when you find love you'll know
it's real

Removing My Bra

THE SIGNIFICANCE OF DEEP WOUNDS AND THE SCARS.

BATTLE SCARS

Yes, there are times you play through the pain. That's life.

When the game ends you have to address those wounds and injuries in order to function properly

Otherwise, they will become infected and cause internal damages and the scarring will be much worse

That's life, when we are hurt, because that is a by-product of life, you will endure some pain

If we don't address or even acknowledge the hurt, bad habits, insecurities and limiting beliefs hinder us from the abundance that awaits us on the other side of our healing.

TRAPPED LIGHT

Perfection is not a requirement to gain access to God's promises. Amen

CONTRACT

I no longer want to give myself (time, energy, or money) to unhealthy habits.

I get myself in situations and circumstances I'm begging God to get me out of, without changing the thoughts and behavior that put me there in the first place.

Because you are not truly ready for the change you seek.

More than breaking bad habits, I never want to break anymore promises to myself.

Breaking the bad habits will help me keep my promises.

Wasting time usually looks like playing games, scrolling on social media ,or sleeping the day away. Not being productive also takes shape in spending time with people who don't feed your goals in life. One of my bad habits was believing I had time. You know the deadline, even ones I set for myself, are so far away I have plenty of time to meet them. Then it's the day of the deadline and guess who's not even close to done. ME.

My mom would say, "A steady drip will wear a hole in a rock." I'd find myself repeating it, but I wasn't so good at taking action on it. She taught it to me when I was struggling to pay bills on time. See, I had the mindset that if I couldn't pay the bill in full I wouldn't pay anything at all. Which only made my late payment even larger and later and would just become an even bigger mountain to move. Which then made me even further behind. Mommy told me if I put something on the bill whenever I could, it would not only get smaller, but in turn, the company could see that I was trying to keep up on my payments and might be more inclined to give me grace and, more importantly, an affordable payment plan.

I've started to apply this principle to other areas of my life as well. For instance, this book. I couldn't write it all in one day, but taking time every day, ok most days, to write at least one paragraph or to write for 30 minutes a day has gotten it done.

With my health, I make a better choice every day to eat healthier. The results are slow but steady. All these small little actions give me back my time, more energy for the things I love, and money to enjoy it. Taking care of myself is profitable beyond the dollars.

Becoming the best version of myself is not some big action I need to take and, poof, all is right in the world. It's the small deliberate actions I take every day, throughout the day. The Bible says it's the small foxes that spoil the vine. Don't let little things creep in and destroy your harvest.

All my efforts involved taking care of other people. Loving them, providing for them, and making sure they were pleased. Never stopping to take time for myself. I was left with the scraps of my time, energy, and money. I realized self-love is not selfish. You can't pour from an empty cup.

Yep, depleting your own resources is an unhealthy

habit. It builds resentment and makes you ineffective for the next assignment God has coming your way. Your day-to-day actions are building your forever. What you value is what remains.

BATTLE FATIGUE

People tell you to vibrate higher
Show up, invest in yourself
Show you have some skin in the game
So, I climb in the ring ready to fight for my dreams
And I repeatedly get my assets handed to me
It's hard not to feel like a liability
I'm scattered and unsure
What's the next move

Everyone I take seems to be wrong
No matter how well thought out or calculated
I'm blown back
Every time I think I've prepared for the left hook
Bam
Here comes the sucker punch
scattered
distracted
disoriented
stepped up
Got knocked 3 steps back
Then I come with the right cross
And realize I'm losing the fight, not the war

WRONG TRUTH OR WRONG LIE

I used to be a tomboy. Getting dirty playing pick 'em up mess 'em up with all the boys on my block.

Jumping ramps on our dirt bikes, which I cried for. My mom came home on my birthday with a pink Huffy. I was distraught! I cried and cried until she took it back and got me a silver and black BMX dirt bike.

Ironically, I'm writing this the day before my birthday.

Somewhere along the way, I was told "no" or "you can't" enough times that the risk-taking, fearless girl shrunk and closed off her adventurous side. I also believe it was over time. Not one big event that minimized it. Just the life happenings that were small enough for me to miss it dwindling.

The first thought or memory that pops in my mind is my stepmom saying to me when I hung out with guys more than girls on any given day after school or on the weekend, "What you doing around them? Being a slut, you gone end up a hoe. Keep it up." Or, when I hung out with a bunch of my favorite girlfriends "Oh you a lesbian now? You wanna be a dyke?"

Wrong = that's all I heard, or should I say carried with me, as I grew up. Everything I do is wrong.

If I got good grades, I thought I was better than somebody.

When I got bad grades, I was a dumb or stupid bitch. Still, wrong.

I realized this week that most times there's no right or wrong. Only your truth. This book is me telling mine.

Sitting down with my thoughts, pain, and triumphs, overcoming, and spilling it all out into something that I pray will change lives.

PICK YOUR POISON

People spouting off about being woke or how sleep somebody is or isn't.

Knowing self is so much more than that.

Hell, I didn't have the time, nor the luxury to learn about my blackness or culture connections.

I was too busy staying safe, or trying to anyway, to see the me my ancestors wanted me to see.

Mentally processing, drugs in my home, my mom in an abusive relationship, going to school to learn and eat one of my meals for the day, then being given two new sets of guardians with a whole new set of abusive distractions. I couldn't be sleep or woke for that matter. I had to survive!

These things were not lost on me: racism, inequality, or sexism. I was a decent student and consumed books. However, to be learning about or finding a course around race or culture wasn't my calling. Healing was.

VALLEY GIRL

I'm the woman who will show you how to get the victory in the valley.

The power that I own despite the poverty that said I never would...

BEING

As the bandages unravel more of my true identity is revealed.

Nothing is too hard for God, but sometimes just *being* can be the most difficult thing you've faced or done.

> Being present
> Being still
> Being vulnerable
> Being open
> Being true
> Just being you
> It's the best, but it's not always easy.

Writing this book, is me just being me, but it's one of the toughest things I've ever done.

Sliding Off My Panties

WHO GOT IN THEM AND HOW,
THE EMOTIONAL AND (MENTAL)
EFFECTS OF EACH EXPERIENCE.

SLEIGHT OF HAND

Like a serenade, his lies fell on me. Hitting my skin like fresh dew in the morning.

Whispers of pain and poor choices wafted through the room. I was enjoying the calamity of all the adults who guided me before. He was speaking their language. It was like French to me, romantic and enticing. What did I know? I was 12. He was 18. Those new parents they gave me, fostered his need to satisfy an urge. Their trust ignited his lust. My voice had been taken long ago, so how could I say it was wrong. His body was warm, like my tears. I found comfort in it. At least I thought that's what he was giving. Instead, as he came, he took. He planted his seed, and from it grew the vine that tangled me up in mistaking attention for love. The fruit of this moment must've been a super food based on its shelf life. Decades of longevity, negativity, and insecurity. I believed I was giving the men what they wanted, never considering what I needed. For so long, my identity was wrapped in this moment. Not knowing I was deity, having full reign over my body and my life.

LABOR PAINS

I wanted a fresh start. New things, thoughts and outcomes

Today, 2 months later I realize that I am experiencing the labor pains of said desire.

Becoming a better version of yourself sounds amazing. All spiritual and harmonious. It is spiritual and you will finally get in harmony with your aligned purpose, but just like the 9 months of gestation you go through mental, physical, emotional and spiritual changes. You are different in ways beyond your current comprehension, just like the new title of mom.

You look and live different. Despite wanting to get back to your pre-pregnancy body you look in the mirror and ask yourself and onslaught of questions. I had to answer a few on my evolution to wholeness. Who am I now? What is true for me now? A mom of adults, a woman finding her true self, owning her power, standing in her truth and unlearning all the limiting beliefs and bad habits that were hindering me from showing up in the world fully. What moves her now? How does she want to move in the world? How will she affect change? What does making an impact look like for her now? See how the questions just come rolling in?

Pushing through those limiting beliefs, Chile listen. Self doubt and self sabotage took me down through there. It takes time to get through these moments. Unfortunately, it can be much longer than nine 9 months. That's not necessarily a bad thing. It just needs to be acknowledged that you in fact need more time. Seeing that we are constantly evolving with each season of our lives be sure to give yourself as much grace as necessary to be whole and free of self imposed guilt or shame. Yes, you may start to send yourself on a guilt trip. Not celebrating victories no matter how small. Exclaiming you shouldn't be excited because this is what you "should've" been doing all along. Hiding your success because others around you are not on the same journey you're on, so you start shaming yourself by hiding in plain sight. Not talking about how well you're doing now because of the changes you've made. Don't leave your love on the shelf, especially for yourself. You've worked too hard to hide for anyone. Bring that new you out into the light for the world to see, enjoy and benefit from.

There is beauty, joy and squeals on the other side of these labor pains. The results will speak for themselves. You've done the work. Bask in it.

CHOCOLATE CHIP COOKIES
VS. OREOS

Maybe I made the choices with men I made because I was still identifying as the little girl that had been taken advantage of by predators instead of the woman who overcame the trauma.

Do you have a favorite cookie? Me, I'm partial to chocolate chip cookies. Especially fresh out the oven. There's something special about a warm chocolate chip cookie.

It took me some time and courageous conversations to realize there is nothing wrong with me. I just wasn't their preference. Like my favorite cookie, when offered options, I prefer it over any other cookie. Just like the men who hadn't chosen me weren't in fact saying anything was wrong with me. I just wasn't what they preferred most. I'm still warm, sweet, and appetizing there was just someone who they preferred most.

For some time, I had internalized their choice as a deficiency in me. Upon further investigation, yes, those courageous conversations, I found that in fact they had not been equipped to digest the delectable sweetness that flowed from my heart and the mental strength I shared to empower both them and myself.

I revisited the trauma because I believe it was easier to stay in the pain than to choose me and change the behavior that kept me settling for cookies I didn't even want. Your comfort zone goes beyond your career choices. It was familiar. I knew it. Beyond the comfort of my trauma, I also didn't really believe I deserved the love I truly desired. So, settling meant I didn't have to come up with the right recipe to heal and get to enjoy the sweet taste of victory.

The same way the men that had crossed my path chose differently so could I. It started with choosing me.

THE FIRST

His name doesn't matter. He was what mama called a
    family friend
So he came with built-in trust
What he offered, however,
Was this toddler's introduction to lust
I can still remember the darkness in his home,
On his lap
With sweaty oily skin
He played the GENTLEman
He was as slick as his skin
He'd slide me back and forth without anything going
    in,
But I could feel "him" growing
Right before my mother's eyes
He was enjoying me,
Pretending to bounce me on his thighs

TRUER WORDS NEVER SPOKEN

When a man (someone) told me I was too good for them, my normal response was to encourage them and build them up. What I should've done was listened, thanked them, and walked away.

This is some huge, major insight.

Joy lining.

I don't have to live in fear of others' opinions of me.

No more settling.

MAC 'N' CHEESE AND CORNBREAD

I settled with food like I did with men. What was appetizing and looked good or gave me comfort, I put in my body.

See what I did there?

Things and people that look and make you feel good are not always good for you.

Just like too much rich food leaves you carrying unnecessary weight, the people left me with unwanted baggage I needed to unload in order to be free to move through life in the freedom I longed for.

Cornbread is my favorite food. Mac 'n' cheese is a close second. As much as I love cornbread, I can't live off of it daily. It would leave my body in a deficit.

Over the last few years, I gave up diary. I know right. NO CHEESE. It wasn't easy at first. My love of cheese for a while was much stronger than I thought. However, eating it was doing a number on my allergies. This is gonna get a little TMI but I need to make this point. The over production of mucus was causing me to choke in my sleep and on some occasions, puke. So, when I weighed how it made me feel AFTER I ate it versus how yummy it tasted WHILE eating it I gave it up to feel my best in the long term.

I think you see where I'm going with this. I started choosing to say no to men that were just appealing and not what would benefit me long term to invest my time in. Being it romantic or friendships. Seeing where it's going doesn't take years. Dead end friendships are also a hinderance even if you feel lonely. Reciprocity is a requirement for friendship. Not tit for tat. Just a mutual experience of give and receive. This requires honesty.

First with yourself, then with the other party.

The other important factor I have to share is that I no longer wanted to wake up feeling the guilt of letting God down the morning after. The walk of shame has nothing on the conviction I felt whenever I went to pray after I'd left someone sheets. I didn't need anyone to condemn me, I had that covered. So, I had more courageous conversations and shared my truth to live guilt free. If there were any missteps (sexually) I had to own them without feeling like I had betrayed myself by never sharing my truth in the first place. In this moment I knew the work I had been doing all these years was taking even more root and I would be the woman and one day wife I needed to be for the husband God is sending my way.

Eye candy is nice but a well-rounded meal with a treat is better.

DAZED AND CONFUSED

When their fingers, among other things, are inside you, there's a slight discomfort. Both mentally and physically. Your mind, heart, and body are at war, except it comes across as dazed. You know it's not supposed to be this person no matter how much you trust them. The boyfriend-girlfriend dynamic is not what's happening here. Just because your body responds one way, doesn't make you wrong. What's happening to you isn't even wrong. Who it's coming from is what's wrong. This moment creates a mental break. Kinda like a page break. In this moment you start rewriting history. Telling yourself it's your fault, that's all they (male or female) want from you, you're bad, all the things that begin a dialogue with your inner self that slowly, day by day, silences the true you.

Physical connection is the second-most intimate connection God designed, and when it is misplaced, the author of confusion rejoices. The only thing that kills his joy is us returning to Love. The creator knows who and what we were designed for. No matter how many dings, dents, or breaks, we encounter, God's desire and intention for our lives remain. When we return to Love, it's like returning back to factory setting. They, the molester, was vying for power. When we return to Love, we take ours back. We remove the grip of shame and free ourselves from the weight of other people's pain.

SCHOOL CLOTHES

As a teenager, getting ready for school is just thinking about what's clean and doesn't require any ironing.

Well, on this day me and my sister made a deal about getting ready. We didn't do laundry on time, so the deal was, she'd put the clothes in the washer, then I'd put them in the dryer. The catch? It was after our bedtime.

The plan was going off without a hitch. The laundry room in the basement could be heard from our bedroom so we knew the washing machine had stopped. I tiptoed down the stairs and put the clothes in the dryer.

My brother was over on his side of the basement, unbeknownst to me, masturbating. When I started toward the stairs he said, "Let me show you something right quick." When I got closer, he said, "Sit down on the bed."

I said, "I had to get back upstairs before I get in trouble." He convinced me no one was awake and it was fine. In my mind, I knew it wasn't fine.

Before I knew it he was under my gown and inside me. My heart and mind were resisting along with my arms and legs. The rest of me, however, made it all confusing as hell. Fight-stay-no fight-why is he so pleased-fight-stay-this is wrong-stay-no no no fight.

As I rip myself away and run for the stairs in my Vaseline-smeared gown he's grabbing at, about four stairs up and away, I'm met with a hard slap across the face.

"If you had your ass in the bed none of this would've happened. Now get in that damn room and go to sleep," spewed from my stepmother's lips.

The clothes felt just as awkward on my skin the next day at school.

When I play this moment back in my mind my thoughts go everywhere. Even as a teenager who knows right from wrong I feel betrayed by my body. Then to be slapped as if you acted alone and no consequence given to the aggressor confirms you must be wrong. The depth of this scar still permeates my life as an adult. Not in a crippling way but being reminded of the pain I was in during this time.

These words are for any other young lady or now grown woman carrying the story of a sexual abuse encounter. Whether it be molestation or rape. No matter if by someone you trusted or a stranger. You are not wrong. You deserve love and physical touch in a safe, trusting, consensual manner.

Every day I do my best to never let this moment steal my freedom. The freedom of forgiveness. Yes, forgiveness. I never have to spend time with or around this person. So why let them or this moment continue to plague my life and future. A future that God has planned with love and abundance.

I know what some of you may be thinking, if God has such great plans for my life and yours why would this happen to me or us. The sovereignty of God is unknown and unmatched. What I believe is that He allowed it to shed light on the brokenness in my life, family, and the world. By telling my story and healing process I now will be able to heal others and their families all over the world. Often times we see good things as the only right things. That's not always the clear view. Sometimes we have to find or become the good thing that came from a bad situation.

F- THAT!

Albeit I'm extremely flattered, I'm over the whole being somebody's freak, but never their forever. This goes way beyond taking my clothes off. It's more about what lies beneath the sensual skin I'm so comfortable in.

I sold myself a bill of goods. The running tally of thoughts about who I was told I'd be vs who I was and what I had to offer where two very different people. I lead with my body because my introduction to intimacy was tainted with lust and other peoples' pain.

I return to what we believe. I was operating off my experiences. No one had told me I could and would have other experiences. That I was entitled to OWN my body. That my ideas and opinion did in fact matter. I put on display what I thought men valued most based on my current experiences. Man, I was hurting. I'm so grateful to be Free.

ANGER BE DAMNED, THIS IS RAGE

A complete waste of time is what you are...
No, please do not try to explain
It makes my ears bleed the pain your words cause
I hate you is too good for you
All the bullshit you have fed me makes me want to be
    anorexic
You make me wanna devour you whole
And regurgitate your bones and feed them to my dogs
They say misery loves company but from now on
I'm going stag
You will no longer get the pleasure of my presence
Hatred is not the word I would use to describe what I feel
    for you
Detest, hell, loathe is more like it
You should give back your balls
Because you should be stripped of your manhood
They say hell hath no fury like a woman scorned
If you happen to cross my path and meet my rage
Hell will be the Hilton compared to the destruction
I plan to bring to your reality
Ignorance should be your job title
Because you have mastered dumb shit
Time is more valuable than money
And plenty of both of mine you have wasted
You just wrote a check your ass can't cash

So sodomy will be your reward
I'm sure somewhere in your childhood you heard it is
      not wise to fuck over a woman
So now this wise woman must break you down
Because of your childlike actions
I would like to decapitate you and like a roach
Have you crawling around for 10 days in torment
Until I finally decide to squash you!!

VIRTUAL ORGASM

The caress of his hands left fingerprints on the keyboard
    of my pores
As text commands of his touch began to form data
    entry
My motherboard accepted his username and password
Along with kisses to my breast
His voice prompts fed my microprocessor
Giving instruction to which components of my body
    would receive the next step in this moment of cyber
    sensation

To allow the intensity to fill my RAM
Yes, my memory with constant pleasure
I closed my eyes all the cards booted up
And video of my dreams began to play in real time
The sound card played audio of the gentle whisper of
    his name and delicate moans of ecstasy
All my systems were networking to create the output of
    my climax
He fused his hard drive with my drive controller
And my controller didn't blow the job of controlling his
    hard drive's operation
As the job was processed with concentrated focus
The information spit out was stored in a file named
    uvula subtitled **back of the throat**
As the operator checked the monitor
He could see a reboot was necessary before he could
    insert his disk in the CD-ROM
He used the disk clean up tool to free up space to give

the computer more juice
To click start, the clit was the start
To be thorough
In and out the tool went
Removing any unwanted programs left by other
    corrupted files
And as cream began to run
The box became open
The clean manager was complete
The clit was ok
I mean click ok
System check was done
And he was ready to see how this software would
    respond to his disk manipulation
He broke the security of my firewall
My files started a meltdown on his hardware
What I was felling had me search the control panel
    to delete all other user accounts and accessibility
    options
The device manager had all operating systems
    performing at full capacity
No syntax errors found
The ease of access center was producing an overload of
    orgasmic messages
Fantasy Reality Erotic And Kinky
As the positions went from one graphic design to
    another
the body of work was a creative production of sensual
    gratification
Log off
Shut down
Hibernate
Sleep

Taking Shoes and Socks Off!

ORDERED STEPS ARE NOT
ALWAYS PRETTY
JUST LIKE FEET.
DOESN'T MEAN THEY WEREN'T
MADE BY GOD,
YOUR DESTINY AWAITS,
FIRST STEP IS TO HEAL,
NEXT IS TO HELP.

YOU & THEM

Everyone is on a journey, just as you have come to the knowledge and understanding you have, allow others that same freedom of learning.

Be the leader you know you are!

Your words should help people tap into their pain to heal, not cause more.

God whispers, "I require your heart for your purpose. The destructive behavior revealed to you in others is the universe revealing yours to you."

Pay attention.

Be your version of beautiful, always.

There is no pedestal, only purpose.

SAVED AND BOUND

Saved and bound.

You're free and you don't know it or are not living it.

The visual God gave me is the elephant that had been cut loose from their chains, but never moved.

The freedom you seek is trapped in the illusion of your conditioning. You are living in the lie of not being enough. It's not just that you were told whatever you were told, you're not enough, you won't be anything, no one will love you, you're not smart… it's that you believed it. Even if it was subconsciously engrained in your membranes, it remains.

You are free.

That's it.

What needs to be answered, is do you believe it.

I didn't.

As a little girl, before I knew God, I prayed that something bigger than me would keep me. He did. Yet, I stayed. I stayed in the pain He had freed me from even though the chains of hurt, betrayal, and abandonment had been broken.

No matter how pretty someone dresses you up if all you see is the ugliness of your past nothing will change.

I wanted to be free. I wanted to feel love. I wanted to enjoy the life I had asked God to give me. My conditioning wouldn't let me until I gave it over to Him. Until I took a long hard look within, I would never uproot the devastation that had taken place in my heart and mind.

I had to make the still small voice of Jesus louder than the one of all the people who spoke or touched me negatively.

It's work to get this wisdom. It's work to be free. Not performance to earn salvation but taking action to be whole. Unraveling yourself from the bondage of trauma to walk in the purpose of the pain. I value the healing I have now. I know I matter to God and that affords me the freedom I live in today.

NIP AND TUCK

Nip and Tuck.

Nipsey Hussle — "keep those who matter present of mind and close."

Everyone is talking about the marathon mindset and the marathon continues. That's great, we should be playing the long game in everything, especially life.

Speaking as a former cross country and distance track star. There is no marathon without being present in the current moment. You're in what I would call a dual mindset (focus). Your goal is miles ahead, so every move is calculated to obtain that goal. Which means you have to be present. Watch your breathing — that's most important. You don't want to faint or hot box because you were sucking too much or not enough air.

Your pace should be steady, going too fast will have you burnout quick and barely putter across the finish line

Run your race!

That's huge.

My coach always told us you're in your lane. That's it! Stay in your lane and focus on your race. Looking around is a distraction. It causes missteps. It chops your steps, that's only good in hurdles which means you know the obstacle is coming.

Staying focused on your race is being present on another level.

When you're present the finish line is all you see

Sure footed, calculated, practiced steps (pace) is what's driving you to your next win

Did you notice that? Practiced steps. You can't win a marathon you don't prepare for.

Period.

So, if you feel like you've done this already or it's taken a little longer than you thought, good! Because that just means when you hit your stride, you'll be able to maintain it and kick up speed on the straight away and win on your terms!

CAN I GET AN UPGRADE?

Lord,

Am I being safe or am I being wise?

At times we know our why. Why we do what we do and why we don't or won't.

Contemplating a new role currently. Moving up, a possible promotion. It will require more of me, more of my time. Consuming more of my life for something I don't love or desire to do. All the times I've said no, that's what I think about, how I can't get my time back. However, the opportunity keeps presenting itself.

I thought to myself, I know my why, well why not, but I hadn't considered God's why. Despite how I "feel" about it, what I think are all the reasons I wouldn't do it, perhaps God has called me to it. Maybe I've been asking the wrong questions and at times, of the wrong people.

First question I asked was, "Let me see the me you see," and He's answered, in fact, He's still answering, which is how I believe I arrived at the question that created this chapter.

The me He sees is a life-changing leader. The me I've been shrinks, hides, only shining when absolutely necessary. Perhaps fearing something I was called to change. Looking back now I wonder how it was possible to shine and dim my light at the same time. Hiding mostly from myself.

I listened to a sermon that mentioned the quality of your questions.

He said upgrade the quality of your questions.

Example: "Not, how can I afford this, but, Lord, who do I need to become to afford it?"

Seeking wise council is first seeking God. Then have Him lead you to the person or people to discuss it with if necessary.

CHECKIN' THE BOXES

I want to experience life on a level I never gave myself permission to enjoy.

The evolution of me is one that I believe is and will be my greatest adventure.

WALK LIKE AN EAGLE

The chains have fallen off.
Now I'm just trying to learn
how to walk in this new freedom.

TO THE ARTIST

I want to visit your imagination
Where creativity resides and logic whispers
Where inspiration sings to the melody provided by
    possibility
As the intentions of your heart
Are displayed with the remnants of your soul
I want to enjoy what spills upon your canvas
With the motivation of intensity
Bursting with bold vibrant colors
That scream, I cannot be contained
I want the articulation of your freedom
To consume me
As it caresses all my senses
With a tenacious grasp
I want the volatile fiction to create
To elevate me to multiple levels of greatness
Where I am suspended in animation
Strung along by wisdom
My robust laughter
Is what your comedic genius is after
Through the tears of my joy
The ingenuity of what you have sculpted
Takes my eyes on a visual exploration
My palate is pleased with tantalizing textures
From your culinary masterpiece

As your words wiggle through my eardrums
The impression of sensual stimuli, change
Hope, deliverance, joy, and peace
Are left as residue on my consciousness
My appetite for great music
Modulates with every performance
As I feast on the eloquence of your vocal style
I hunger and thirst for the artistry of your brilliance
That of which you have let me partake
And sharing my gifts and talent
Will forever be an expression of my gratitude

JUST ADD TAX

What I've had and what I deserve
have been two very different things.
I'm coming to collect!

ONE AT A TIME

Does mindfulness eliminate multitasking?

If you are fully present and focused on and in the moment, multitasking is a distraction.

FATE

Fate

*F*orever

*A*ligned

*T*o

*E*ternity

RESURRECTION

How I live and the permission I was seeking may be a good way to examine my power in choices.

Things and opportunities have come to me and I've said yes, which have shaped the life I've lived.

This thought came to me today after a friend texted me to go for a morning walk for our exercise today, and I accepted.

Now, at this time I don't have a vehicle, so it was great to get in a workout that wasn't in my bedroom and alone.

But the above thought lead me to thinking about all the times I've said I'm tired of just existing. I want to live.

I feel like I have been, living that is, I've said yes to new things that this journey called life has brought me to. My steps are ordered, so God knew the woman I am today before she knew herself. So the excitement I thought I'd need to have what a "lived" life looks like may be a false truth I was telling myself I needed instead of truly seeing my life for the gift it has been in its divine beauty. Creating excitement and a well lived life looks different to the one living it.

If a librarian is surrounded by books and that is their love and passion, to them their life is exciting. Same for a chef or novice foodie. A good new recipe tried every week is bliss.

If what you say yes to fuels you no matter how minuscule or grandiose, it's your joy that feeds it and fills you up.

EVOLUTION REVOLUTION

You have this idea in your head of what personal growth and change will look like.

Well, at least I did.

You think when the shift comes it's gonna be glorious and miraculously beautiful. Harmony and cute little birds are gonna sing while you evolve.

Instead, it feels like death. Yes, things are dying from within, but you literally feel the grief. The pain of letting go, ditching old habits, and removing people, places, and things that no longer serve me feels like death of a loved one, you, meaning me, hear the triggers, and the tears start to stream

The more you clear away, the more sensitive you become. You're emerging.

The infancy, the genesis of walking in your true power. It's new, so you stumble a little, getting your bearings, so why would you think you'll have it all together or be perfect?

Cry, feel, move in your authenticity. The more you do it, the stronger you will be.

Purpose is helpful (inhale).
Perfection is control (exhale).
Authenticity over comparison.

WEED WHACKER

When the old you is dying, be careful, the pain and discomfort will make you want to retreat back to the poor behavior, either because it's familiar, you're seeking validation instead of growth, or fear has overwhelmed you due to the isolation.

Regrets — or the thought of things you've done to yourself or with other people — will have you saying things like "How stupid, why did I go there, why didn't I use self-control?" You have to just remind yourself that was the old you even if it was yesterday.

Clearing away inner clutter is a unique eye opener. Especially when it has you resting.

I am clearing out to give the work, my family (children), and clients the best version of myself and an exceptional exclusive experience.

Clearing away the chaos that I may better serve all.

Everyday I'm striving to be a better me. To see. To know. Where I'm going and how to get there.

WHY I SPIT

I spit because a friend introduced me to it
Like heroin in a syringe
I needed to do it
Again and again
It was my inoculation
To a lifetime
of endless
Possibility discrimination
I spit, because pissing on
People's intelligence
Would just be rude
I drop knowledge
But no one pays attention
Unless it's Victoria's secret
Being revealed to some dude
Yes sometimes when I spit
It's smooth, succulent, and soft
Some of what I spit
Even makes me wanna get off
Just because my lyrical lust game
Arouses most
Doesn't mean
I wanna spit on every post
You may ask why I spit
It's my liquid asset
And one day
Cash will come in from it
As an entrepreneur
What I spit

Will be infused in all I do
Returning as legal tender
For me to stand on
Spitting is a therapy for me
Tears flow better as words
And someone out there
Needs my pain to be heard
You have your theory on
The history of 2 C
But you have no idea
Of what's in a name
Triple threat
Does not fret
At what you've spat
A human dictionary is cool
But not always where it's at
Simplicity over
Encyclopedia Britannica vocabulary
Is what some say
My flow is
The essence of poetry
I've been told by one of the greats
My metaphor game
Is sick with it
And
No matter how you see me
I will continue to spit it
This may not be my best work
Or your favorite piece
But I will keep spitting
Because my body
Cannot contain
What my mouth
Wants to release

Dropping Accessories

THERE WILL BE TITLES, TOYS
AND TRADITIONS THAT MAY
LOOK NICE AND AT TIMES
MAKE YOU FEEL THE SAME
WAY, BUT THEY ARE NOT THE
CORE OF WHO YOU ARE OR
WHAT YOU WERE PUT HERE TO
SHARE (SHOW OFF)
SO BE SURE NOT TO GET
THROWN BY THE GLITTER
AND GLAM,
BUT INSTEAD BE SURE GOD IS
GETTING THE GLORY.

MIRROR

Have you ever been in a place where nothing is going right, but all seems right and the peace you feel is incredible?

When you grow, even when falling forward, into your new normal, letting go is as important as grasping the future. The unlearning is really what's unnerving. Letting go of controlling the outcome and not letting the unknown overwhelm you is the true work.

Peace is found here.

REALLY, THOUGH?

Asking God for help is one thing but receiving (accepting) it from who He sends to give it is something else.

That's the work: letting go of how it's supposed to be fixed or what the outcome should be versus what God's will is for all involved.

POWER PLAY

Wisdom without action is just hope, not faith.

Aligned power applies pressure to the problems keeping you from practicing the process that executed God's plan, which will have you live out your purpose.

YOUR TRUTH

Even if you can't figure out who you are, remember whose you are.

He will lead you to all truth, even the truth about you.

HIDING IN PLAIN SIGHT

I have been talking "to" myself not "about" myself when I write. I don't notice that I'm even sharing outward even when I speak of myself.

I have disassociated myself with the success and significance God says I deserve.

I was watching my life instead of showing up as me.

Writing like I'm talking to a friend instead of saying my, me, and I.

My distance from this abundance stems from a lack of self-worth I hadn't been honest with myself about. I talked a good game but didn't believe what was for me would not pass me by. What we say and know don't manifest until we believe it.

My depersonalization, I now know it as such, was I believe a protection from all the let downs and betrayal I faced up until now. If I saw these moments as "someone else's" when they didn't come to pass the disappointment was also someone else's.

However, no matter how much I mentally distanced myself, the regret was still 100% mine and fully experienced by all the parts of me.

HIS

Called
Made in His image
Born
Neglected
Molested
Changed
Sister
Friend
Smart
Strong
Removed
Fostered
Terrified
Stronger
Raped
Reunited
Duped
Abused
Fortified
Raped
Mom
Graduate
College student
Lost
Survivor
Sinner
Fiancé
Alone
Free
Salvation
Pain

Courageous
Loner
Grace
Career
Dismayed
Connected
Adored
Grateful
Giving
Devastated
Estranged
Open
Changing
Trusted
Writer
Entrepreneur
Excited
Loved
Family
Hurt
Change
Abundance
Growth
Movement
Developed
Mentored
Detailed
Late
Evolved
Warrior
Homeless
Rescued
Leader
Conqueror
Overcomer
President
Supervisor
Refined
HIS

GOD'S VIEW

Vision 2020
My voice
My values
My victories
Matter for Gods vision of my life

Rinse and Reflect

SHOWERING YOU WITH LOVE
AS YOU CLEAR YOUR HEART
AND MIND OF WHO YOU
THOUGHT YOU WERE SO YOU
CAN STEP INTO WHO GOD
CALLED YOU TO BE.

ACKNOWLEDGMENTS

Since I can remember I've loved putting pen to paper. No genre or structure, just writing. I literally love it. English was my favorite subject in school. I still graduated writing like I talk though. Also, I am a Pen Snob. Reeling that my pens and paper created a published book! This proves to me God knows from the beginning and uses it all.

I asked You to keep me. I asked You to protect me. I asked You why. I asked You to give me favor. I asked You to give me peace. I asked You to show up. I asked You to show out. I asked You to love me. I'm grateful You did just that. God you are my all and all. I'm thankful for our relationship. I'm grateful You don't ask me to be perfect, just faithful. Not only would this book not be without You. I wouldn't be the woman I am today without You. Thank You, Lord.

Jennifer Tuma-Young my publisher and founder of Inspired Girl Enterprises. What a ride! We are just getting started. Number one is in the books! Our friendship is truly divine. I am forever grateful God brought you across my online path. Offering me the opportunities to share my light in ways I've dreamt of for years. I'm grateful and excited to create more light bearing projects.

Allure and Soul Photography this cover… The photoshoot was work surprisingly. I wouldn't come out my shell. Regardless, you nailed it. You got my initial concept. However, your eye (your wife's creativity) and them angles, changed the entire look and turns out it's a hit. And they say don't hire friends. Thanks again for everything!

My village who has held me down and lifted me up on many occasion. My heart is full from your support of listening to my story and then encouraging me to share it. Most of you were there when the pain was too real. Gail Renee: Oh the things we have talked about over a cup of coffee (and some glasses too wink wink). This love so deep is now rooted in sisterhood. The first friend my kids call auntie. Your pep talks in the early stages of writing this book still play in my head with each new thing I embark on. I'm so thankful for you. Big Mama: I'm so thankful for your heart for my family. It made penning these words much easier pulling from the wisdom you've shared with me over the years. Auntie Jen: Thank you for never letting me be disconnected from my biological roots. I'm so grateful for our hours on the phone, praying, laughing and encouraging each other. Tara: for always telling me to believe in me. In my ability, my talent and worth. For seeing me when I wasn't looking deep enough. Thank you for being a big sister from another mister. Oh and for teaching how to drive LOL. Tracy: To say biggest supporter would be an understatement. If my name has been on it you have been at it or bought it. I value the calls and text that encourage me on every endeavor. There are so many others I could name, but then that would be another book. Thank you all for your continued love and support.

My Daddy. The coolest man I know. I'm so grateful to see you with empathic eyes and a forgiving heart. Thankful that we work at our love between father and daughter. I light up with every phone call knowing I'm going to hear the joy in your voice telling me you love me and how proud you are. I'm grateful that God is not bound by time and that as long as He has given you more of it, anything is possible.

Hey Mommy. I believe you're proud. Some of these stories we discussed and some I'm sure you would've never wanted for me. I'm thankful that God redeemed the time and gave me back the eight years I thought I lost while in foster care. I'm glad I got to experience more of the healed you. It gave me the tenacity to keep typing when I wanted to sleep or do anything but write. Thank you for loving yourself and God enough to return to me in adulthood. I miss you dearly and I know there will be another mommy daughter reunion one day.

To the two people who initiated my leadership skills, my little brothers. Your unwavering love for me helped me write this book. Hell, it helped me survive this life that is written in this book and the rest of the stories to come. Daniel: The first of my little big brothers, we have some unspoken truths we share. I feel them when we hug. We don't talk daily, but I know you're a phone call away if and when I need anything. Same. You were my first friend. I'm thankful we are still close. Thank you for trusting me when we were both lost. I love you Dee. Tellious: For your nonstop expression of the value you find in our relationship I have no words. When I thought I failed you, there you were celebrating me for being your guide. Seeing me beyond my flaws and failings cheering for my greatness to fully manifest, there you are. The time is coming for us to build together. This sibling duo coming with disruption in business and biblical execution. I thank God He kept us for such a time as this. Let's ride! I love you Tee aka Fatty. Thank you both for loving me and encouraging me to be great always.

To my babies, whew. Thank you for seeing me as more than your mommy. I am so blessed to have been chosen as the woman to guide your lives and bring you here. You're all grown now and embarking on your own journey of healing. Growing together has been one of the greatest bond building experiences with each of you. Thank you for the laughs, the dance performances, the music games we made up and everything else that kept me sane and focused while creating for the world. Thank you for always supporting me living! For riding with me when things looked grim and celebrating when they got better. My first review panel for everything, including this book. We have so many more stories to share with the world. I pray I'm around to see how yours continues to unfold.

CoCo (Me) - You did it girl! Yep, go ahead and cry. It's ok. You did that! You didn't SHRINK! It's a whole book out here with your face on the cover! I'm so proud of me!! For bringing my whole self in the room. For bringing all the messy and all the miraculous to the light. I wanna thank me for being brave, resilient, vulnerable and willing to evolve.

RESOURCES

If you or anyone you know are experiencing any form(s) of abuse here are some resources that may be helpful:

HOTLINES

National Sexual Assault Hotline:
1-800-656-4673

Substance Abuse Hotline:
1-800-662-4357

National Domestic Violence Hotline:
1-800-799-7233 or SMS START to 88788

Suicide and Crisis Lifeline: Call or Text 988

Here are some tools and resources
that helped the author on her healing journey~

BOOKS

Woman Thou Art Loosed Bible by T.D. Jakes
The Four Agreements by Miguel Ruiz
The Year of Yes by Shonda Rhimes

PODCASTS

Myleik Teele with Myleik Teele
Woman Evolve with Sarah Jakes Roberts

APPS

Insight Timer
First 5

AND...

Prayer
Meditation
Drink Water
Mind Your Business

(Romans 10:13 NKJV). "That if you confess with your mouth the Lord Jesus and believe in your heart that God has raised Him from the dead, you will be saved."

ABOUT THE AUTHOR

Niccole Nelson is a thought leader, speaker, writer, and coach. The owner of NiccoleNelson.com, she is using her light and love for people as a change agent in every room and industry God sends her to. She has maintained a twenty-seven year postal career, nine of those years in management. As Board President of the neighborhood she grew up in as a foster child, she led her team and the organization in raising twenty+ million dollars over seven years. Niccole's life mission is to help people see themselves as valuable and equip women with the tools to heal from trauma to use their voice in the world. She currently lives in Detroit along with her three children.

CONNECT WITH NICCOLE

CPSIA information can be obtained
at www.ICGtesting.com
Printed in the USA
JSHW080727280423
40985JS00005B/20